Exploring Niagara

Exploring Niagara

The complete guide to Niagara Falls and vicinity

Hans and Allyson Tammemagi

NIAGARA PENINSULA CONSERVATION AUTHORITY

OAKHILL PUBLISHING HOUSE

Canadian Cataloguing in Publication Data
Tammemagi. H. Y.
    Exploring Niagara : the complete guide to Niagara Falls and vicinity

Includes bibliographical references and index.
ISBN 0-9681815-0-3

1. Niagara Falls Region (N.Y. and Ont.) - Guidebooks.
I. Tammemagi, Allyson, 1947- . II. Title.

FC3095.N5A3 1997   917.13'39044   C97-930170-X
F1059.N5T35 1997

Graphic design by Campbell Creative Services, St. Catharines, Ontario
Editing by Torrance Publishing & Editorial Consulting, Thorold, Ontario
Colour separations and printing by Lincoln Graphics Inc.,
    St. Catharines, Ontario

Oakhill Publishing House
P.O. Box 22012, Glenridge Plaza
St. Catharines, Ontario L2T 4C1
(905) 641-2732 Fax: (905) 641-1705
oakhill@vaxxine.com

Dedication to Sponsors

This book would not have been possible without the generous support of our sponsors. *Exploring Niagara* is dedicated to our sponsors and all the people who share our vision of Niagara as one of the most fascinating, diverse and beautiful places in the world.

The Steering Committee for the Niagara Gateway Project

Vintners Quality Alliance

Niagara Credit Union

Niagara Economic & Tourism Corporation

St. Catharines Chamber of Commerce

Bed and Breakfast Accommodations – St. Catharines & Region

Table of Contents

EXPLORING NIAGARA
The Complete Guide to Niagara Falls and Vicinity

Chapter 1

WELCOME TO NIAGARA

From the earliest days of the exploration of North America, there was a story told by the Indians of a mighty waterfall hidden in the middle of the continent. They painted a picture of immense volumes of water frothing over a cliff and crashing with a mighty roar on the rocks below.

One can only wonder at how the explorers felt when they first discovered Niagara Falls. In that remote untamed wilderness, surrounded by primeval forest, veiled in an ever-present mist, and with the crashing of water echoing through the woods, the Falls must have inspired a profound reverence and awe.

The mighty water fall became known as Niagara, an Indian word meaning "The Strait," although the more colourful "Thunder of Waters" is also recognized. Today, the cascading waters of Niagara Falls are considered by many to rank among the seven natural wonders of the world and are one of the top tourist attractions in North America.

Like a prima donna, Niagara Falls has captured centre stage and has made it difficult to see beyond the glare of the spotlight. However, those that take the time to look beyond the Falls will discover that within about 30 minutes driving time there is a wealth of other fascinating attractions ranging from natural beauty to history to engineering marvels. Indeed, the Niagara area is one of the most diverse and rich areas in the North American continent. Sadly, most visitors to Niagara do not see far beyond the glamour of the Falls and miss many of the other treasures. But what are those other treasures, and how has this area been formed?

More than any other force, water has been dominant in moulding the character of Niagara – water that tumbles over the Falls, water that flows through the Niagara River, water that carries ships through the Welland Canal, and water that resides in the Great Lakes of Ontario and Erie. This water offers moderation against the harsh inland climate and falls gently and abundantly on the land. Combined with the mineral rich soil, this has led to a verdant land with bountiful orchards and vineyards.

The churning waters of the Niagara River provide power. In the early days, the fast flowing water turned mill wheels. Niagara Falls was the birthplace of alternating current which allowed the transmission of electricity over great distances and opened up the modern electrical era. At the turn of the century, the power of the Falls seemed limitless. Today the mammoth hydroelectric generating stations on the Niagara River are amongst the largest in the world and provide power for a significant part of northeastern North America.

The Welland Canal, which was constructed to link Lake Erie with Lake Ontario and offer ships a safe detour around Niagara Falls, has a long and colourful history. It has also had, and continues to have, a profound influence on the area. Hours can be spent watching ocean-going ships from distant countries slowly raising and lowering their way through the locks, looming large over the landscape, bearing their cargoes to and from distant destinations.

Niagara is also shaped by its geog-

Map 1, The Niagara Region

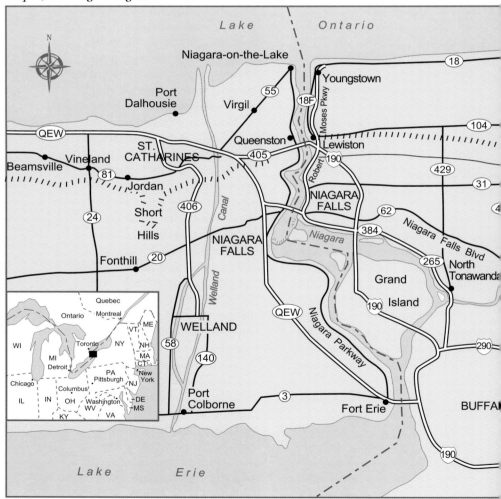

raphy. The Niagara Escarpment, the cliff that forms the edge of the plateau over which Niagara tumbles, stretches like a backbone in a long east-west line through the Niagara area. Protected by law against development, it is a last bastion of nature in an area that is rapidly becoming urbanized. Tucked away in this long strip of Carolinian forest and limestone cliffs are small, delightful waterfalls that cascade over the escarpment edge, mimicking the mighty Niagara.

History has stamped its indelible mark on this area. Because the Niagara River forms part of the vital artery joining the Great Lakes to the Atlantic Ocean, it has played a strategic role in the development of North America since the earliest days of exploration. Explorers have walked here, soldiers from three nations have fought to control this territory, politicians have set up legislatures and passed laws, and engineers have constructed tunnels, canals, and power stations.

The purpose of this book is to draw all of these things together under one cover and offer visitors and residents alike a comprehensive reference to exploring the rich Niagara mosaic.

The emphasis is on getting out and learning about Niagara by travelling its back roads, hiking its trails, leaning against a fence or bar and exchanging gossip with locals. *Exploring Niagara* encourages everyone to get active and drive, bike, and walk through this wonderful area.

A walk or a tour means so much more if you understand the circumstances, the history, and the reasons for why things are the way you see them. Such an understanding opens up totally new perspectives that make a tour much more enriching and enjoyable. We have tried to capture, both in text and pictures, the dramatic history and rich background of the area so that you may glean this "deeper" perspective.

We hope that *Exploring Niagara* will not only be carried in car gloveboxes, bicycle panniers, and hikers' backpacks, but will also be pulled from the bookshelf, perhaps on a winter's eve, to reminisce in front of the fireplace about places you experienced or to seek out sites that you will "discover" next time.

How to Use this Book

Exploring Niagara presents more than 50 tours and places of interest in the Niagara region. All of these are located within about 30 minutes drive of the Falls and sites on both sides of the border are included. The Niagara region is shown in Map 1. There is considerable diversity in these tours, and they can each take from less than an hour up to several days.

Each tour is usually presented with a map, a description of how to get there, and the highlights that are to be seen. Note that there are tours that can be taken by car, by bicycle, or on foot. In many cases, a single tour can be done by two or even three of these methods, depending on how much energy and time you have. Do not look upon our suggested tours as cast in stone. On the contrary, use them only as starting points and modify them to suit your own tastes and schedules.

Those who are unfamiliar with the Niagara area may wish to read Chapters 2 and 3, which describe the history and natural setting of this region, respectively. Following that, the tours are grouped by the main geographic feature that is described. Each of the following has an entire chapter devoted to it: Niagara Falls, the Niagara River (one chapter for each side of the border), the Bruce Trail, the Welland and Erie Canals, and so on.

Each chapter provides a brief background on history and other noteworthy details about the area, then suggests some tours. Simply choose the one(s) of interest and

follow along; they are self guiding and self explanatory. Any facility that charges an admission fee is indicated by a dollar sign in brackets following its name; for example, Fort George ($).

Please note that our focus is on presenting tours that describe the character of Niagara. For this reason, we have not included Casino Niagara, amusement parks such as Marineland, water slides, wax museums, or similar attractions. Brochures describing such attractions are available at hotels and travel information centres or by contacting the organizations listed in the Appendix.

A list of festivals and major events is provided in Chapter 17. These range from re-enactments of the War of 1812 to crafts fairs to wine festivals.

The index is a handy tool. If there is a place that interests you but it is not listed by main chapter, you can look it up in the index to see if there are any tours nearby.

A bibliography is included for those that wish to do additional reading.

Organizations that can provide additional information, such as tourist information centres and chambers of commerce, are listed in the Appendix. These organizations will be pleased to assist you.

Chapter 2

FLORA, FAUNA AND FOSSILS

For the nature buff, Niagara, in spite of its relatively small land mass, is a captivating area, and countless days can be spent rambling and exploring its rich diversity of landforms and living things. Old wooden barns, moss covered stone walls, crevassed cliffsides, and delicate water falls are hidden like treasures amongst the Carolinian forests of maples, beeches, oaks, walnuts, and tulip trees.

Landform and Geology

The landform of Niagara is dominated by the Niagara Escarpment, a craggy, fossil-rich ridge of dolomite that traverses the entire region. Its north facing cliff forms a prominent spine that offers topographic variety to what is otherwise a relatively flat and monotonous landscape.

But what is the escarpment and how did it form? The Niagara Escarpment is a landform known as a cuesta, that is, the flank or slope of a hill. In simpler terms, it is a ridge composed of gently dipping rock layers with a long, gradual slope on one side and a relatively steep scarp on the other side.

The Niagara Escarpment rises near Rochester, New York, and then runs eastward through the Niagara Peninsula along the south side of Lake

White-tailed deer

Ontario to Hamilton where it bends north and extends to Tobermory on the north end of the Bruce Peninsula. From there it crosses to Manitoulin Island and then westward across northern Michigan and down the west side of Lake Michigan into the state of Wisconsin. This feature is the outer rim of a large saucer-shaped basin which is centred in the state of Michigan.

The escarpment was shaped by geologic forces acting many hundreds of millions of years ago when the North American continent was still young. About 470 million years ago rivers flowing into a shallow tropical sea carried sand, silt, and clay that were deposited in thick sedimentary layers to form the Michigan Basin. Simultaneously, lime-rich organic material from the abundant sea life was also accumulating. Over the eons, these materials became compressed into massive layers of sedimentary rocks such as limestones, shales, dolostones, sandstones and reef structures that can now be viewed in the walls of the Niagara Gorge and along the escarpment.

The ancient sea began to withdraw about 300 million years ago forming a large plain. Over the succeeding millions of years the plain, subjected to immense subterranean forces, buckled and formed into a saucer-shaped basin. At the outer rim of the basin, erosion slowly removed the softer shales that lay under the more resistant dolostone layers (dolostone is similar to limestone but magnesium replaces some of the calcium). As the softer underlying material was eroded away, large blocks of the more resistant overlying dolostone broke off, creating the vertical face of the escarpment as we see it today.

The escarpment is a geologist's paradise, containing some of the best exposures of fossils from the Upper Ordovician and Silurian geologic periods (about 470 to 410 million years ago) found anywhere in the world. Suggested geologic outings are presented in Chapter 15.

Water

Successive advances of glacial ice sheets over the last two million years have dramatically altered the escarpment face. They have widened and deepened valleys and carried rock debris many kilometres and then deposited them in massive moraines. A picturesque example of the handiwork of the ice age is at Short Hills, where running water combined with glacial erosion has left a jumble of small hills and valleys, which are now punctuated by winding laneways and tucked-away cottages.

Water is ubiquitous in Niagara. There are long shorelines on the north and south, the mighty Niagara River carves a channel through the heart of the region, and numerous rivers, creeks, and marshes offer refuge for wildlife. For example, Wainfleet Bog, over 1,200 hectares (3,000 acres) in size, is one of the few major wetlands left in southern Ontario and is home to numerous rare

Geology of the Niagara Escarpment

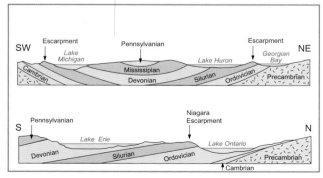

Wetlands at Chippawa Creek Conservation Area

species of animals and plants.

Water flows over the escarpment creating waterfalls that range from the mighty Niagara Falls to wispy delicate veils. Erosion at the headwaters of the numerous streams is largely responsible for the many indentations and irregular appearance of the escarpment face. The most spectacular effect of the erosive power of running water is the Niagara gorge, which has been carved a distance of about 11 kilometres (6.8 miles) in the past 12,000 years by Niagara Falls, from Queenston Heights to its present location. A hard top layer of dolomite limestone is underlain by softer layers of sandstone and shale. The shale and sandstone are eroded by the roaring Niagara waters until the top limestone layer is sufficiently undermined to collapse. This process maintains the vertical face of the

Falls, preventing it from becoming a series of rapids.

Until the early 1950s, the Falls eroded at the average rate of 1 metre (3.3 feet) per year. Since then, the

Climate Facts
Average Daytime Temperatures

January:	-1°C (30°F)	July:	22°C (72°F)
February:	-2°C (28°F)	August:	22°C (72°F)
March:	2°C (36°F)	September:	17°C (63°F)
April:	8°C (46°F)	October:	12°C (54°F)
May:	15°C (59°F)	November:	5°C (41°F)
June:	19°C (66°F)	December:	1°C (34°F)

Average Annual Rainfall: 70 cm (27 inches)

Number of Days per Year with Some Sunshine: 300 days

major hydroelectric power projects, Sir Adam Beck 2 on the Canadian side and Robert Moses power plant on the US side, have lead to the diversion of a considerable amount of water from the Falls. In addition, the

International Control Works now spreads the flow of water more evenly over the entire crestline of the Horseshoe Falls. It is estimated that the erosion rate has decreased to about 0.3 metres (one foot) per ten years, or about 3% of what it was previously.

Climate

In spite of its northerly latitude, the Niagara area has a moderate climate because of the presence of Lake Ontario and Lake Erie. The lakes also contribute moisture for the abundant rainfall that soaks the fertile soils.

White-tailed Deer

The white-tailed deer is one of the largest and certainly one of the most elegant mammals in the Niagara area. A doe usually gives birth to one or more spotted fawns in late May or early June. The doe and fawn stay close together for about four months. During fall, deer tend to herd up in groups and often spend the winter in dense protected parts of the forest called "deer yards." With a home range of between 40 and 80 hectares (100 and 200 acres), deer occasionally wander into residential areas to sample garden foliage.

Flora

The advances and retreats of glaciers have left a legacy of rich soil, particularly below the escarpment where previous glacial lakes have covered the bedrock with thick layers of soil. Combined with the moderate climate, this is one of the most fertile areas of Canada as witnessed by the bounteous orchards, vineyards, parks, and nurseries.

The Niagara area is in the northern-most part of the Carolinian Zone, which extends from the coastal zone of the Carolinas northward between the Mississippi River and the Appalachian Mountains just reaching into southern Ontario. Compared to the massive size of Canada, the Canadian Carolinian Zone is very small. Altogether, it represents less than one quarter of one percent of the total land mass. However, it is an area that is characterized by tremendous variety, with more rare species of plants and animals found here than in any other part of Canada. In 1894, the chief gardener of the Niagara Parks Commission conducted botanical studies and found 909 separate species of flowering and fern-like plants growing in the vicinity of Niagara Falls.

Over 70 species of trees are found in the Niagara area. Although many evergreen species are present such as pine, spruce, cedar, and hemlock, the woods are dominated by deciduous trees consisting largely of broad-leaf hardwood species such as sugar maple, beech, red oak, white oak, and bur oak. Other species include black walnut, sycamore, white oak, shagbark hickory, and rock elm. The occasional tulip tree, black cherry, magnolia, black oak, and paw paw are also found.

Shrubs that are common in the Niagara area include dogwoods, high bush cranberry, common elder, staghorn sumac, and the scratchy raspberry.

Plants that are typically Carolinian include purple bitter cress, sandbur, Carolina spring-beauty, horse-balm or stoneroot, yamroot, white trout-lily, swamp rose mallow, yellow stargrass, spike blazing star, yellow flax, wild lupine, Virginia blue-bells, broad beech-fern, and pokeweed.

Vines also thrive in this area including the Virginia creeper and riverbank grape. Herbaceous plants and weeds include the New England aster, evening primrose, and butterfly weed. Many thorny and thistle-bearing plants are also encountered and will leave their mark on hikers who wander off the trails.

Fauna

The diversity of vegetation provided by the Carolinian forest provides bountiful food and habitat needed to sustain wildlife. Over 50 species of mammals inhabit the escarpment area. Grey and red squirrels, chipmunks, skunks, raccoons, and mice are common. Mammals that are seen somewhat less frequently include red foxes, bats, coyotes, mink, weasels, muskrats, and white-tailed deer.

Niagara is a rich environment for birds due to its wealth of habitats

Predators
The fox, opossum, skunk, and racoon live in a wide variety of Niagara habitat. The skunk and racoon also include urban settings as part of their domain, to the frustration of many home owners. These animals have a wide-ranging diet that includes carrion, small birds, frogs, insects, mice, berries, and nuts. By culling weak and diseased animals, preying on rodents, and scavenging carrion, they perform a valuable service.

including wetlands, conservation areas, and the escarpment. Over 300 species of birds have been identified in this area. Year-round residents include grouse, chickadees, woodpeckers, and cardinals. Spring and summer residents are robins, barn swallows, and various warblers and vireos.

Frequently sighted birds include horned and pied-billed grebes, great blue herons, American bitterns, Canada geese, mallard, wood and canvasback ducks, ring-necked pheasants, kildeers, spotted and least sandpipers, herring and ring-billed

Birdwatching at Beamer Conservation Area

NIAGARA PENINSULA CONSERVATION AUTHORITY

gulls, common terns, ruby-throated hummingbirds, blue-jays, mourning doves, red-winged blackbirds, robins, red-headed, downy, and hairy woodpeckers, common crows, common grackles, and many species of wrens, warblers, swallows, and sparrows.

Often turkey vultures, red-tailed hawks, sharp-shinned hawks, sparrow hawks, and owls can be seen nesting along the escarpment. A spring-time ritual for birdwatchers is the hawk migration at Beamer Conservation Area in Grimsby. At this highest point of the escarpment, thousands of red-tailed hawks, as well as eagles, vultures, and falcons, gather to prepare for the long flight across Lake Ontario to their summer nesting grounds.

Nowhere else in Canada are there more species of reptiles (27) and amphibians (20). It is a delight to see turtles sunning themselves on a partially submerged log on a summer's day. The area is home to 50 species of spiders and insects not found elsewhere in the country.

Fish

The most important fishery in the area is Lake Erie, which contains smallmouth bass, yellow perch, yellow pickerel (walleye), and northern pike. Lake Ontario sustains a smaller, but still significant, sport fishery with rainbow trout, chinook and coho salmon. Rainbow trout, chinook and coho salmon, and smallmouth bass are found in the Niagara River.

Turtle enjoying the sun

NIAGARA PENINSULA CONSERVATION AUTHORITY

Chapter 3

A STEP BACK IN TIME

The Early Days

The early days in the Niagara area were peaceful and serene – a striking contrast to the blood-thirsty wars that were to follow. Archaeological studies indicate that the Niagara area has been inhabited by native people for approximately 8,000 years. The earliest recorded inhabitants were the Neutral Indians, a peaceful woodland culture who formed a buffer, or neutral area, between the warring Hurons and Iroquois.

By about 1650, the Neutrals had been largely annihilated by the Iroquois, or Six Nations Indians, a much fiercer and more war-like tribe. The Iroquois lived in villages of long houses and were able to maintain relatively permanent villages as they had developed basic farming skills and grew beans, squash, and corn. Fish was also an important part of their diet. The Iroquois were cruel and fierce fighters who terrorized the neighbouring tribes and were much feared by white settlers. Because of the threat to their territory, Iroquois warriors became involved in and played an important role in the War of 1812.

The white man's interest in the interior of Canada was largely motivated by the lucrative fur trade that followed water ways from the Atlantic Ocean up the Great Lakes. Situated on the major water artery leading inland, Niagara Falls was destined to be discovered in the early days of North American exploration.

Although other white men undoubtedly saw the Falls earlier, the first European to record his visit to

> ### First Impressions
> *"This wonderful Downfal, is compounded of two great Cross-streams of Water, and two Falls, with an Isle sloping along the middle of it. The Waters which fall from this horrible Precipice, do foam and boyl ... making an outrageous Noise, more terrible than that of Thunder."*
> *These words were written in 1678 by Jean Louis Hennepin, the first European to record his impression of Niagara Falls.*

Niagara Falls was the Frenchman, Father Louis Hennepin, who visited the Falls with LaSalle in 1678. Hennepin was overwhelmed by the majesty and grandeur of Niagara Falls and described it in his book *Nouvelle Découverte*.

The French were the first white explorers in this area and established forts to protect the fur trade. In 1721, a trading post was established at Lewiston, which flourished under the expert guidance of Louis Joncaire. In 1726, the French constructed Fort Niagara to guard the Lake Ontario entrance to the Niagara River. To allay the concerns of the Indians, the Fort (see Chapter 6) was disguised as a French chateau. With its massive stone walls, this is the oldest remaining building in the entire Great Lakes area.

With control of the Niagara River and a network of forts stretching from Quebec to Detroit, the French were masters of the Great Lakes. The Niagara River was the gateway to a vast, rich inland empire built on the lucrative fur trade.

The British, however, also had an interest in North America and were chagrined by the success of the French. They brought mounting pressure to bear on Fort Niagara and in 1759 laid seige. When a troop of French reinforcements from Buffalo were defeated, the commander of Fort Niagara surrendered, marking the end of French influence in the Niagara area and also the beginning of the end of French power in North America.

The American Revolution brought more upheaval and fighting to the Niagara region. Fort Niagara become the base for British raids against the American revolutionaries, and Butler's Rangers and their Indian allies made sorties far into what is now New York State. Niagara-on-the-Lake was originally named Butlersburg in honour of Colonel John Butler who led the Rangers.

The peace treaty following the American Revolution in 1783 saw an international boundary drawn down the middle of the Niagara River, so that Fort Niagara came under control of the United States. However, British troops continued to occupy Fort Niagara until 1796 when Jay's Treaty was negotiated for its return.

First Settlement

Settlement of any serious nature did not occur in this area until a flood of United Empire Loyalists arrived during and after the American Revolution of 1775-1783. They were attracted particularly to Niagara-on-the-Lake, which was founded as Newark in 1781, because of its proximity to the USA. Starting as a military base and haven for Loyalists, Newark grew rapidly in the late 1700s. Because of its strategic location, it was named capital of Upper Canada (later to become the Province of Ontario). In 1792, Lieutenant-Governor John Graves Simcoe convened the first parliament of Upper Canada there. With the return of Fort Niagara to the Americans in 1796 there was grave concern over the proximity of the capital to the American guns, and the capital was moved to York (later to become Toronto).

The War of 1812

When the War of 1812 erupted, the Niagara area was one of the main battlefields. The legacy of that last great conflict between our two nations remains today in the form of historic forts, monuments, cemeteries, and other memorials. In June 1812, the US Congress declared war on Britain with the aim of quickly capturing Canada by attacking on four fronts, one of which was Niagara.

On October 13, 1812, American forces from Fort Niagara crossed the Niagara River from Lewiston and captured a position at Queenston Heights. The invaders were repelled with heavy losses, but in the battle, the British lost General Isaac Brock, whose memorial is seen today towering over the escarpment.

A few weeks later, on the other side of the Niagara Peninsula, the Americans abandoned their efforts to capture Fort Erie after a few skirmishes. However, on April 27th, 1813, an American force attacked and captured the town of York (now Toronto), the capital of Upper Canada. In retaliation, the British later burned Washington.

The Americans next mounted a major offensive. After a heavy barrage of Fort George and Newark by over 70 cannons from Fort Niagara and the American fleet, an attack was successfully launched causing the British to retreat toward Hamilton. The fortunes turned, however, as the Americans were defeated in a night battle near Stoney Creek. Another troop of American soldiers, sent to capture a British strong point at Beaverdams, was ambushed after the British had been warned by Laura Secord of the impending attack. Laura Secord, who walked over 32 kilometres (20 miles) through difficult terrain to deliver the news, has become a national heroine. Her house has been made into a museum and can be seen in the Village of Queenston (see Chapter 5).

The Americans continued to occupy Newark and its surrounding area. But the conditions that winter were difficult, and doubting their ability to hold Fort George against an attack, the Americans withdrew to Fort Niagara on December 10, 1813. As part of their withdrawal, they set Newark ablaze. Only one of its 150 buildings was spared.

On December 19, 1813, British forces crossed the Niagara River and captured Fort Niagara, which they held until the end of the war. The British then marched south and burned Lewiston and Manchester (later Niagara Falls, NY).

At the other end of the river, a different tune was to be played. In the summer of 1814, an American army

Laura Secord Monument at Queenston Heights

crossed the river and easily captured Fort Erie. Heading north, they won a subsequent battle at Chippawa.

Three weeks later, the armies met again at the Battle of Lundy's Lane, the bloodiest and most bitterly fought engagement of the war. Both sides suffered heavy losses, and although both sides claimed victory, the American offensive was halted.

A few weeks later, a determined British offensive on Fort Erie was repulsed by the Americans. Although they held Fort Erie, the Americans were unable to break out and gain further ground. Finally, the American forces blew up the Fort and retired to Buffalo, marking the end of active warfare on the Niagara frontier.

Why West Point is Grey

The reason why West Point cadets wear grey dates back to 1814 when American forces defeated the British in the Battle of Chippawa in the War of 1812. Due to a shortage of supplies, none of the regular blue uniforms were available and the army had to march to battle wearing grey instead. Legend has it that in honour of this victory, West Point cadets today wear grey.

The War ended in December 1814 with the signing of the Treaty of Ghent, and after all the blood letting, very little had changed – the armies were effectively back where they started.

The Freedom Trail

On May 21, 1793, the first parliament of Upper Canada convened in Niagara-on-the-Lake and passed a bill prohibiting the introduction of further slavery into the country. As a result, Upper Canada became a haven for black Africans who had been sold into slavery in the United States. From the 1820s onward, about 40,000 black freedom seekers followed the North Star to Canada via the so-called Underground Railroad. The Niagara area was an integral part of this path to freedom and a substantial population of blacks established itself in the Niagara region.

To commemorate Niagara's role in the Underground Railway, a series of plaques have been erected at a number of historically significant sites including one in Fort Erie describing the ferry system that aided many of the escaping slaves to cross the Niagara River, another at Bertie Hall, Fort Erie, which was used as a safe house, and another at the Negro Burial Ground at 494 Mississauga Street, Niagara-on-the-Lake. A book and a brochure entitled *Niagara's Freedom Trail* are available from the Niagara Economic & Tourism Corporation (see Appendix). These describe the history of the Freedom Trail as well as a tour of these black heritage sites.

The Great Ditches

After the War of 1812, the development of the Niagara area proceeded again. Now talk arose, on both sides of the border, of replacing the portages around Niagara Falls with a canal. Soon afterwards, the sounds of construction rang across the Niagara frontier as the Americans began digging a giant ditch. The Erie Canal was a visionary engineering project that linked the Niagara River (just north of Buffalo) to the Hudson River. The

The second Welland Canal in downtown St. Catharines, circa 1870

Canal allowed access to the Atlantic Ocean via Albany and New York for the growing American settlements in western New York and in the upper Great Lakes. A Lockport resident, Jesse Hawley, first introduced the concept of the canal, and in 1817, the state legislature, led by State governor DeWitt Clinton, authorized its construction. The digging of the 363 mile (585 kilometre) ditch began in 1821 and was completed on October 26, 1825. Almost overnight, the Erie Canal brought prosperity to Buffalo, which became the jumping-off point for the interior of the United States.

Today, the Canal is used primarily for pleasure craft rather than commerce. A more detailed description of the Erie Canal is found in Chapter 8.

The success of the Erie Canal lead to agitation for a canal on the Cana-

dian side of the border. With the War of 1812 still fresh in their minds, the government was not enthusiastic to build such a strategic canal so close to the border. Thus, it was left to a Canadian businessman from St. Catharines, William Hamilton Merritt, to build the first Welland Canal. Although his Welland Canal Company was not financially successful, it did complete the canal in 1829. In 1841 the private company was dissolved and the government took over.

The Welland Canal has undergone considerable improvement since the first one with its 40 wooden locks. The current canal, the fourth one, and using only eight locks, was completed in 1932 and follows a nearly direct north-south route from St. Catharines in the north to Port Colborne in the south. The canal has

Mill district, circa 1890

had a profound influence on the Niagara area. Previously, settlement had concentrated around Newark and was primarily agricultural in nature.

Nikola Tesla

Nikola Tesla was a visionary who invented the alternating current system, which is the basis of electric motors and the long-distance transmission of power. In the late 1890s, he was the most celebrated scientist in the world and today he is remembered by the unit of magnetic induction, the Tesla. Born in Croatia in 1856, he immigrated to the USA in 1884. In 1891, he sold the patents to his alternating current dynamos, transformers, and motors to George Westinghouse who, in turn, was awarded the contracts to install electric power machinery at Niagara Falls. Westinghouse went on to build a megacorporation based on Tesla's genius.

Busy ports were located at Queenston, Lewiston, and Chippawa to portage around Niagara Falls. These communities declined and new communities such as St. Catharines, Welland, and Port Colborne sprang up along the line of the waterway, along with considerable industrial development.

The Welland Canal, at 32 kilometres (20 miles) long, is the third largest canal in the world. Together with the other locks that form part of the St. Lawrence Seaway system, it opens up the interior of the continent to the largest ocean-going ships in the world. A more detailed description of the Welland Canal is found in Chapter 7.

Harnessing the Power of Niagara

Even as early as the 1700s, entrepreneurs dreamed of harnessing the vast power of the Niagara River. The first to do so was an entrepreneurial Frenchman, Chabert Joncaire, who used a waterwheel to power his sawmill just above the American Falls in 1757. The first major tapping of Niagara's power did not occur until the late 1800s when Jacob Schoellkopf, a Buffalo businessman, constructed a canal which supplied water to a number of factories on the American side of the border. By 1882, seven industries were linked to the canal and operated machinery through hydraulically-powered shafts and pulleys. Schoellkopf also built a small powerhouse on his canal and supplied power to 16 street lamps in Niagara Falls, New York. However, the full potential of Niagara could not be unlocked until a means of transporting the power to larger industrial centres like Buffalo and Toronto was available.

The key to sending high voltages to distant places along slender wires was alternating current, which was invented shortly before the turn of the century by Nikola Tesla. In 1895, the first large-scale hydroelectric plant in the world, the Adams Station, began operating in the gorge using alternating-current generators designed by Tesla and George Westinghouse. A year later the power was transmitted to Buffalo along cables. In 1903, Schoellkopf constructed another hydroelectric plant on the lower river.

With Niagara's genie released from the bottle, the next decade saw Niagara Falls, New York emerge as the centre of the electro-chemical and electro-metallurgical world. America had thrust itself into the electrical age.

Canada was much slower to harness Niagara's power, but in 1905, the Canadian Niagara Power Company, wholly owned by Americans, produced electricity, most of which was transmitted to the US. A year later the Toronto Power Company and the Ontario Power Company

The amount of water that can be diverted for power generation is specified in the 1950 Niagara Treaty between the USA and Canada. During daylight hours of tourist season, the flow in the Niagara River must be more than 2,830 cubic metres (100,000 cubic feet) per second. At other times the flow must exceed 1,415 cubic metres (50,000 cubic feet) per second.

began to generate electricity. The Toronto Power Company's power house, situated on the banks of the river above Horseshoe Falls, is a neo-classical palace with massive stone pillars extending along the entire front. Known locally as the Engineerium, you will see it in Tour 2, Chapter 4.

A number of other relatively small, in comparison to today's standards, power plants were constructed in the vicinity of Niagara Falls.

The generation of power not only was an enormous boost to industry but also gave birth to a wonderful tourist attraction. The electrically-driven Niagara Gorge Railway started from Niagara Falls, New York, and descended into the gorge via a long grade. It then followed the edge of the river past the Whirlpool Rapids to Lewiston. It was later extended to cross the river near the Queenston-Lewiston bridge and climbed the escarpment near Brock's monument and followed the top of the gorge back to Niagara Falls, Ontario. This railway carried millions of sightseers and operated until 1933 when the ever-present danger of rock slides finally caused the "Grandest Scenic Trip in the World" to pass into history.

The full electrical potential of the Niagara River began to be harnessed with the construction of the Canadian Sir Adam Beck power stations and the American Robert Moses station. Sir Adam Beck I was completed in 1921 and was at that time the largest hydro power station in the world. Water is brought to this site via a canal from the Welland River near where it enters the Niagara River about a kilometre (0.6 miles) above the Horseshoe Falls. The second power station was completed in 1954 and receives water from above Horseshoe Falls via large tunnels that pass under the City of Niagara Falls.

On the opposite bank of the Niagara Gorge is the large American power station Robert Moses, which was completed in 1961 and has a capacity of 2,400 megawatts. In total, the Niagara River generates about 4,400 megawatts of electricity. Together these mammoth stations along with the smaller stations near the Falls divert through their turbines a considerable quantity of water that would otherwise cascade over Niagara Falls. So if you think the Falls appear bigger in the daytime, it's not an illusion caused by too much Niagara wine. Instead, this "illusion" is caused by the power stations, which consume about 50% of the river's flow at night time and during the non-tourist seasons.

Recent Years

In the past few decades, the older industries of this area have had problems maintaining a competitive advantage and have declined. This has been off set to some degree by the growth of tourism. Niagara Falls has always been a major attraction, but now there is much more to see and do in the Niagara area including big-name entertainment at Art Park, classic theatre at the Shaw Festival, gambling at Casino Niagara, tours of the canals and wineries, and much more.

Agriculture continues to play an important role in the Niagara area due to the fertile soil, mild climate, and abundant rain fall. Fruit orchards are a blaze of blossoms in the spring and yield a bountiful harvest of cherries, plums, nectarines, peaches, apples, pears, and grapes. A pleasant development has been the success of the vinifera grape varieties and the maturation of the wine industry. Many boutique wineries have sprung up, and a wonderful way to spend a day is by touring wineries and sampling their excellent vintages – but more about this in Chapter 11.

Chapter 4

THE MIGHTY FALLS

Niagara Falls is the number one billing, the prima donna, the big splash, the fatal attraction, the jewel in the crown of the Niagara area. It is hard to believe that such a simple thing as water, one of the most basic of elements, can create such a wonder and attract people from around the world. Niagara Falls has been visited by kings, queens, presidents, prime ministers, movie stars, the rich and the famous, and by millions of other people – all seeking a view of this water falling over a cliff.

It is not water in itself, however, nor the height of its fall, that makes Niagara Falls so spectacular. Instead, it is the immense quantity of water. About 50 waterfalls in the world are higher than Niagara Falls, but only one, Victoria Falls in Africa, carries more water.

The rain that falls in the drainage basin of the four upper Great Lakes, a vast geographic area encompassing a large fraction of the interior of North America, collects in the lakes and eventually funnels through the narrow Niagara River on its way to the Atlantic Ocean. Water that is now foaming over the Falls may have fallen years ago somewhere in the rugged wilderness of north-west Ontario, or on the dairy lands of Wisconsin, or the industrial cities of Illinois.

Aerial view of Niagara Falls

Niagara Falls was born in the last ice age when vast ice sheets up to 900 metres (3000 feet) thick covered this area. As the ice receded, the melt-waters left an immense lake, the predecessor of the four upper Great Lakes, perched on a plateau. The water was drawn by gravity and began to flow along what is now the Niagara River toward the distant

Atlantic Ocean. The spot near Queenston Heights where it tumbled over the edge of the plateau became Niagara Falls.

In the intervening 12,000 years, the immense, unceasing power of the flowing water has gnawed away at the rock strata, eroding relentlessly into the plateau until today the Falls are located about ten kilometres (six miles) further back from the escarpment edge. The path that the Falls have taken is clearly marked by the Niagara gorge, a deep gash into the heart of the bedrock. This erosion process continues and every now and again another rock falls as Niagara chews its way upriver.

Table Rock and Clifton House, circa 1860

Early Tourism

Even from its early days, Niagara Falls inspired awe and drew people from around the world. Of course, the earlier tours of Niagara Falls were considerably more exciting than what is encountered today. In 1753, J.C. Bonnefons, one of the earliest recorded visitors to the site, was lured by the challenge of the gorge. Using roots, branches, and rock ledges as footholds, he descended into the gorge near Table Rock. Soaking wet and deafened by the roar, he was able to clamber behind the Falls where he found a cavern the size of a large house. A trip behind the Falls today is just as exciting, but is certainly a lot safer.

The commercialization of Niagara Falls began in the late 1700s when a log hut was erected near Table Rock and served as an inn. Queen Victoria's father, the Duke of Kent, took refreshment at the inn in 1791.

By the early to mid 1800s, the area around the Falls was overrun with a motley collection of buildings and booths that crowded right up to the edge of the gorge. The unwary visitor had to suffer a gauntlet of cabmen, runners, concessionaires, and hustlers who competed unscrupulously for the tourist dollar.

What must be ranked as the most deplorable stunt in Niagara's history took place in 1827. Two hotel owners purchased the condemned schooner Michigan and advertised that it would be sent over the Falls with a cargo of wild animals. As it turned out, the wild animals were two bears, a buffalo, a racoon, a dog, and some geese. Nonetheless, ten thousand came to watch this spectacle. Sadly, only the bears survived.

Hotels along the gorge competed furiously for the tourist dollar and built stairways down into the gorge. The cost of souvenirs, photographs, and going down into the gorge and behind the Falls was often grossly misrepresented. Tourists who balked at these exorbitant prices were threatened and even physically abused. Nevertheless, visitors came in droves to see the Falls.

Not surprisingly, a groundswell of public sentiment arose to improve the conditions at the Falls. In 1885, the Queen Victoria Park Commission, the forerunner to the Niagara Parks Commission, was formed to protect the beauty of the Niagara Falls on the Canadian side. In parallel on the US side, the New York State Reservation at Niagara Falls was formed in 1885 on 167 hectares (412 acres) of land.

Stunters

Like Mount Everest, there is something about Niagara Falls that captures the imagination of the adventurer, and a never-ending parade of would-be heroes has come to conquer the Falls. These daredevils have attempted many kinds of stunts in their quest for their "15 minutes of fame" including tight-rope walking, going over the Falls in a barrel, and swimming the Whirlpool Rapids.

Of all the daredevil stunts that have been performed at Niagara Falls, tightrope walking has captured the most attention and has become a

romantic symbol of the Falls. In June 1859, Jean Francois Gravelet, better known as the Great Blondin, announced that he would cross the gorge just below the Falls on a tightrope. Huge crowds gathered to watch the death-defying spectacle. Incredulous onlookers saw the diminutive Frenchman delicately walk out onto the middle of the gorge where he lowered a rope to the Maid of the Mist,

Funambulist
Tight-rope walker. From the Latin: funis, rope and ambulare, to walk.

raised up a bottle, and then sat down on the thin wire for a quiet drink. On his way back to the Canadian shore, he suddenly steadied his long balancing pole, and executed a back somersault. The crowd went wild.

This immense success was followed by a series of ever more challenging stunts. Blondin was to cross the tightrope on many more occasions on bicycle, blindfolded, pushing a wheelbarrow, with his hands and feet manacled, and with his manager on his back. In one of his most entertaining stunts, Blondin carried an iron stove, skillet, ladle, and various dishes to the middle of the gorge. Balancing precariously, he set down the stove, lit a fire, and with smoke billowing from the smoke stack, proceeded to cook an omelette. Once the omelette was cooked, Blondin lowered it to the Maid of the Mist waiting in the river below where it was served to the passengers.

An almost fanatical rivalry began between Blondin and William

Leonard Hunt, known as Signor Farini. Farini duplicated most of Blondin's stunts and tried to outdo him at every turn. This competition undoubtedly pushed Blondin to greater heights and contributed to the enormous popularity of these spectacles. Although Signor Farini was a superb showman, he never managed to steal the limelight from the Great Blondin.

Many others followed Blondin and Farini in the years to come, but after a fatal accident in 1887, further tight-rope walking was prohibited. The fascination with tight-rope walking was briefly rejuvenated in June 1975 when Henry Rechatin made an unauthorized crossing of the Whirlpool Rapids on the Aero Car cables. His stunt included a crossing on a motorcycle with his wife hanging upside down below the cycle – the ultimate in spousal trust. Today, a statue of Blondin is mounted on a tightrope that crosses Clifton Hill, and provides a glimpse of the bygone era of funambulists.

Over the years, fifteen people have intentionally plummeted over the cataracts sealed inside various forms of "barrels." What is amazing is that only five of these efforts failed.

The first to challenge Niagara was Mrs. Annie Taylor, a 63-year old schoolteacher who decided that a trip over the Falls would earn her fame and fortune. On October 24, 1901, she was strapped into a harness inside a large barrel and was towed into the rushing River. The barrel plummeted over the Falls and crashed into the foam at the bottom. A while later, when the barrel was retrieved on the Canadian shore, Mrs. Taylor emerged, dazed and shaken, but alive. Annie Taylor, who challenged the mighty Niagara, had achieved the fame she sought. Sadly, the fortune was more elusive, and she died destitute 20 years later.

On July 9, 1960, a miracle took place. A seven-year old boy, Roger Woodward, was swept over the Falls without the protection of a barrel – and survived unharmed. The motorboat in which he had been riding capsized and he was swept over the Falls wearing only a lifejacket.

The crew and passengers of the Maid of the Mist were astonished to see him bobbing in the water, and pulled him aboard. Dazed but otherwise unhurt, Woodward recovered and went on to lead a normal life. He occasionally returns to visit Niagara Falls, where his life was miraculously spared.

Even though barrelling over Niagara Falls is now prohibited and the police are diligent in trying to prevent any exploits that might lead to a loss of life, the craze for fame and fortune still continues.

On Sunday, October 1, 1995, a fortune seeker from California adopted a modern approach as he entered the river and raced on a jet ski towards the brink of the Falls. His intention was to discharge a rocket-powered parachute that was strapped to his back and drift gently through the mist to the waters below. Unfortunately, his equipment malfunctioned and the stunt ended in tragedy.

Modern tourism

Shortly after the Queen Victoria Park Commission was formed in 1885, it began to expropriate the land immediately adjacent to the Falls and to make improvements that continue today. In 1885, there were no sanitary facilities, no drinking water, and no safety barrier along much of the gorge bank. Since then, parks and picnic areas, night-time illumination of the Falls, the Festival of the Lights, fireworks programs, and many other attractions have been developed to enhance the enjoyment of Niagara Falls. In 1927, the name of the Commission was changed to Niagara Parks Commission to reflect the broader scope of its mandate, which extended the entire length of Niagara River.

However, the memories of yester-year and the human nature to make a quick buck still linger. In addition to the natural wonder of the falls, you will also be confronted by the gaudy man-made spectacle of wax museums, dare-devil artifacts, houses of horror, and other attractions that are designed to make a hefty dent in your wallet. The focal point of this glitz is at Clifton Hill, the modern-day version of the hucksters and schemers who pursued the tourists of yesteryear.

TOUR 1:
In Awe of the Falls

If you have arrived in Niagara Falls for the first time, there is no better introduction to the Falls than a stroll along the Promenade on the Canadian side that parallels the gorge and goes right beside the thundering Horseshoe Falls. The Promenade extends between the Rainbow Bridge at the north end to past the Horse-shoe Falls at the south end.

The view of the immense cascades and the rocky gorge cliffs is

Journey Behind the Falls

NIAGARA PARKS COMMISSION

Maid of the Mist

breathtaking. The mist thrown up by the crashing torrents often enshrouds the falls and causes rainbows to arc brilliantly in the haze. The tiny Maid of the Mist boats can be seen far below, struggling against the powerful currents and appearing to go dangerously close to the cascading falls. It is worthwhile to repeat this walk after nightfall when the Falls are illuminated and take on a totally different and dramatic character.

Occasional forays across the road are recommended so you can enjoy Victoria Park, which contains some of the finest gardens in the province. From early spring to late fall, park gardeners display an everchanging sea of colourful flowers. The highlight occurs during the last week of April when the park is carpeted with a dazzling array of over 70,000 yellow daffodils.

Oakes Garden Theatre and the adjacent Rainbow Gardens next to the Rainbow Bridge feature a beautiful amphitheatre including attractive formal gardens, rock gardens, and lily ponds. Located on the site of the former notorious Clifton Hotel that burned down in 1932, the amphitheatre suggests the theatres of ancient Greece and has two pavilions that are oriented to provide viewing of the Horseshoe and American Falls. This little area, which is popular for wedding photos, is an often-overlooked oasis of calm beauty next to the hustle of Clifton Hill.

For a close-up impression of the power of the Falls we suggest that you take a ride in the Maid of the Mist ($), which will set your pulse racing and give you a good soaking as the engines roar and the boat bucks and fights against the current and goes practically under the Horseshoe Falls. These tiny boats have been an attraction at Niagara Falls since 1846 and have never lost a passenger. The original Maid of the Mist was a barge-like side wheeler powered by coal-fired boilers and mounted with two smoke-belching stacks. Over the years, the Maids have carried hundreds of thousands of sightseers including dignitaries such as Queen Elizabeth II, Prince Philip, Soviet Premier Alexei Kosygin, Marilyn Monroe, and India's Nehru.

Another excursion that lets you see the immense power of the Falls up real close is the Journey Behind the Falls ($), which takes you from Table Rock House via elevators and tunnels to an observation platform at the foot of the falls and to viewing stations behind the falls.

TOUR 2:
A View of the Falls and Much More (Map 2)
Although a longer walk, this six kilometre (3.7 mile) loop excursion for which you should allow about two hours offers an interesting and detailed look at the Canadian side of Niagara Falls. It is a walk of contrasts, presenting a diverse range of sights and sounds including not only panoramas of the mighty Falls, but also the tranquil beauty of Dufferin Islands, the pell-mell of Clifton Hill, and even a brief glimpse of the industrial side of the City of Niagara Falls.

A good starting place is the parking lot of the Niagara Parks

The Scow
The scow, a landmark in the Niagara River, broke loose from its tug boat in August 1918 with two men aboard and drifted with increasing speed toward the Falls. In those terrifying moments, the men had the presence of mind to open the bottom doors and flood the scow, which fortunately stuck on the shoals. Watched by a large crowd, a life-saving gun was used to shoot a line from the roof of the Toronto Powerhouse to the scow. The lines for the block and tackle of the breeches-buoy became tangled and it took all night before the lines were freed and the men rescued, 19 hours after the ordeal began.

Niagara Parks Greenhouse

NIAGARA PARKS COMMISSION

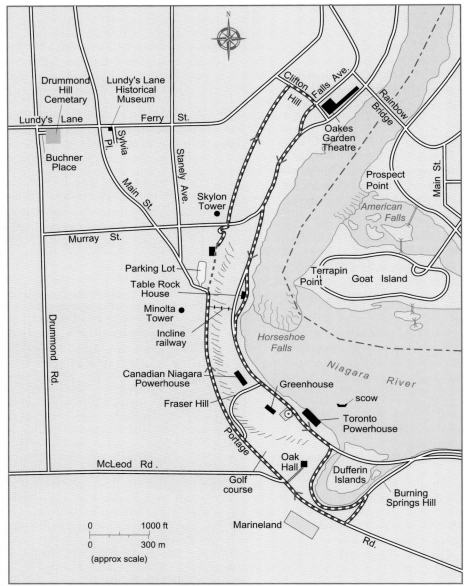

Map 2, A View of the Falls and Much More

Commission's Greenhouse, which is located about 500 metres (550 yards) south of Horseshoe Falls. (Another good starting point, especially at peak season, is the parking lot at the top of the incline railway on Portage Avenue.) A visit to the Greenhouse, where bedding plants for the extensive display gardens of the Parks Commission are grown, is recom-

Toronto powerhouse, known locally as the Engineerium

NIAGARA PARKS COMMISSION

mended for anyone who enjoys the sight and scent of thousands of exotic flowers. Over 150,000 annual and perennial plants from the Greenhouse are planted throughout the park system each year. Unlike commercial greenhouses, the Parks Commission emphasizes unusual species of flowers as well as high quality. One section features colourful massed arrangements of beautifully scented flowers of seasonal interest, such as Easter lillies in the spring, chrysanthemums in the fall, and poinsettias during the Christmas season. Tropical birds live in the tropical section of the greenhouse that features plants from around the world.

Nearby is a Fragrance Garden that contains plants with aromatic fragrances and unusual textures.

Braille plaques allow the visually handicapped to also enjoy this garden. The walkway leading to the Greenhouse is lined with magnolia trees that transform to a shimmering canopy of white and pink with the advent of the spring blossoms.

Proceed south past the Toronto Power Company powerhouse on the left, an Italian renaissance-style

Whence the Name Burning Springs Hill?

In approximately 1794, a spring was discovered near Dufferin Islands that emitted a flammable gas that was venting from the underlying Queenston Shale. An entrepreneur was quick to build a wooden shelter over the spring and captured the natural gas in a barrel with a pipe protruding. For a small charge, visitors could witness the removal of the cork from the pipe and the ignition of the gas. The Burning Spring was apparently the first of thousands of tourist attractions at Niagara Falls and remained a point of interest for over 60 years.

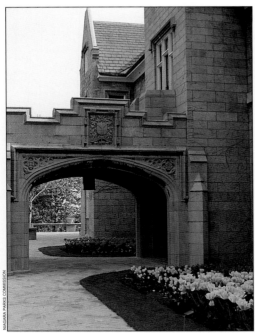
Oak Hall

Go up Burning Springs Hill and turn right at the top. Across the road is Marineland, a popular theme park. Continue ahead keeping to the right. On the right-hand side is Oak Hall and a par- three golf course. Sir Harry Oakes, a prospector who struck it rich, built Oak Hall in 1929 on the foundation of a home originally built in 1805. Featuring 35 rooms, 17 bathrooms, and a basement swimming pool, this Tudor-style edifice was purchased by the Niagara Parks Commission in 1959 and presently serves as its headquarters. The Great Hall reception area, the dining room, and the living room are maintained in their original state and house the Commission's collection of Niagara Falls memorabilia. They are open to the public.

Shortly past the blocked-off Fraser Hill road, a footpath begins that offers lovely views down the hill to Niagara Falls. Enter the parking lot for the incline railway where you will find a pleasant park on its east (river) side with tall trees and large blocks of limestone. Pass through the park continuing north parallel to the river and descend down a small road to Murray Street.

Cross Murray Street and proceed straight ahead and through the Skylon Tower parking lot. Continue ahead, passing through the Venture Inn parking lot to Clifton Hill, the neon and glitz street of Niagara Falls. Clifton Hill is always crowded as people cram to see the wax museums, house of horrors, and other attractions. Turn right and descend to the river's edge and stroll leisurely back

building constructed in 1906 of Indiana limestone. Behind the powerhouse in the shoals of the river is the rusting hulk of a scow that has been marooned there since 1918.

Continuing southward you soon reach Dufferin Islands, a well-known beauty spot in this area. The islands are formed in an embayment of the river and are bordered by high glacial banks. This secluded area features nature trails, picnic spots, and swimming in pools that have formed behind a series of gentle waterfalls. Photographers are drawn to Dufferin Islands in the fall when the calm pools reflect the brilliant foliage. It is hard to imagine that less than 200 hundred years ago this placid area was occupied by an iron foundry and a saw and grist mill.

to the Greenhouse, enjoying the magnificent views of the American and Horseshoe Falls.

TOUR 3:
An American Perspective (Map 3)

Although most tourists flock to the Canadian side for views of the Falls, there is much to see and do on the American side. In 1883, the New York State Reservation expropriated Prospect Point, Goat Island, and other nearby lands to create parkland that would suitably showcase the splendour of Niagara Falls. Since then, numerous other improvements have been implemented.

As shown on Map 3, there are three main areas to visit, and these can be comfortably reached on foot, by car, or by bicycle. No specific tour is recommended. Instead, we suggest you explore the following areas at your own pace.

Map 3, An American Perspective

The first stop is Prospect Point which is adjacent to the north edge of the American Falls and is a prime viewing area for the Falls and gorge. Rainbows can often be seen in the early morning mist, and the Falls are spectacular at night when they are dramatically illuminated by multi-coloured floodlights. During the summer, this is an excellent spot to watch the free fireworks display each Friday evening at 10:00 pm. Prospect Point features a Visitors' Centre, an observation tower ($), gardens, exhibits, and access to the Maid of the Mist boat rides ($).

A ramble through Goat Island and its associated Green, Luna, and the Three Sisters Islands is highly recommended. Quieter and more peaceful than Prospect Point, Goat Island has spectacular close-up views of the waters rushing to the brink of the Falls and is also the terminus for the Cave of the Winds trip ($), which offers guided walks along walkways at the base of Bridal Veil Falls.

The third site is the Schoellkopf Geological Museum (nominal $) which is a short walk north along the river. It can be reached by a scenic footpath from Prospect Point or by driving. The Museum has exhibits and a show that describe the 435 million-year geologic history of the rocks that compose the Niagara gorge and the 12,000 years of the Falls recession from the edge of the Niagara Escarpment. Operated as part of the New York State Park system,

Collapsed Schoellkopf power station, 1956

interpretive programs and walks are also offered.

Be sure to walk up to the gorge viewing platform just off the parking lot. It offers a great view of the Falls and gorge and also provides a reminder of the harsher side of Niagara. Looking down along the stark cliff walls to the left you can see the ruins of the Schoellkopf power station. The two generating stations, which housed six generators, took six long years to construct (from 1918 to 1924) on the site of the former Mill District. The gorge walls were honeycombed by watercourses and wheel pits from the previous flour, paper, and silverplating mills. Although the tunnels for the power station were lined with concrete, they began to leak, causing a major rock failure. The power houses were destroyed in an instant when a rock slide carried them to the bottom of the gorge on June 7, 1956 with the loss of one life.

TOUR 4:
Lundy's Lane Battlefield

An interesting side trip from the immediate Falls area is the Drummond Hill Cemetery in Niagara Falls, Ontario, the site of the Lundy's Lane battlefield, one of the bloodiest battles of the War of 1812 (see Map 2). Friend and foe are buried here side by side in the quiet cemetery.

Also buried here are many early pioneers including Laura Secord and her husband. A number of monuments and markers have been erected to honour the deceased soldiers and pioneers. A corner plot in the ceme-

Laura Secord's grave, Drummond Hill Cemetery

Laura Secord: Canadian Heroine
In June 1813, the 23-year old Laura Secord overheard American plans to attack a British garrison near what is now St. Catharines. From the village of Queenston, she trudged over 32 kilometres (20 miles) through wilderness to deliver the warning in time. Her gallant effort has captured the hearts of Canadians. In June 1901, a special monument with a bronze bust of her as a young woman was erected over her grave adjacent to the Battle of Lundy's Lane monument. The monument can be seen today in the Drummond Hill Cemetery.

tery is reserved for unidentified bodies recovered from the Niagara River.

You may also wish to visit Lundy's Lane Historical Museum, which is located toward the Niagara River from the cemetery at 5810 Ferry Street on the southwest corner of Ferry Street and Sylvia Place in a stone building constructed in 1874.

Chapter 5

FOLLOW THE NIAGARA RIVER: THE CANADIAN SIDE

Sir Winston Churchill, not renowned for lavish praise, travelled the Niagara Parkway and called it "the prettiest Sunday afternoon drive in the world". The Parkway to which he referred stretches for 56 kilometres (35 miles) from Lake Erie to Lake Ontario along the Canadian side of the Niagara River. Recently, a paved recreational trail has been added so this ribbon of gardens, parks, and museums can also be enjoyed by cyclists, walkers, joggers, rollerbladers, and the physically challenged.

The situation, however, was once far from what it is now. In the late 1800s, the area around the Falls was the worst tourist trap in North America, with the banks of the gorge crowded with sleazy sideshows and unsightly exhibits. The criticism levelled by many visiting dignitaries brought demands for government action, and in 1885, the Queen Victoria Park Commission and the New York State Reservation were formed in Ontario and New York, respectively.

The Queen Victoria Park Commission first acquired the land around the Canadian Falls in the late 1800s, and their visionary work continues today under the name Niagara Parks Commission. The Commission now controls almost the entire Canadian shore of the river from Fort Erie to Niagara-on-the-Lake and has transformed it into a continuous corridor of parkland.

Today, the Commission maintains 1,168 hectares (2,888 acres) of parkland and through attractions such as the Spanish Aerocar, the Butterfly Conservatory, and the Journey Behind the Falls, is totally self-funding.

The Parkway between Fort Erie and Chippawa was completed between 1908 and 1915. The section of Parkway between Niagara Falls and Niagara-on-the-Lake was opened in 1923 and provided passage to many areas, such as the Niagara Glen, previously accessible only by railway.

The Parkway is described from Fort Erie northward to Niagara-on-the-Lake (See Map 4). Only main features are described as the tour is virtually a continuous parade of museums, picnic spots, river overviews, grand homes, fruit and vegetable stands, and plaques, which are simply too numerous to mention. These make for a memorable drive or cycle with opportunities for dozens and dozens of interesting stops. Note that it is permissable to pull your car onto the grass in most places along the river side of the Parkway. Thus, you are not restricted to parking lot areas and can create your own picnic spot at any

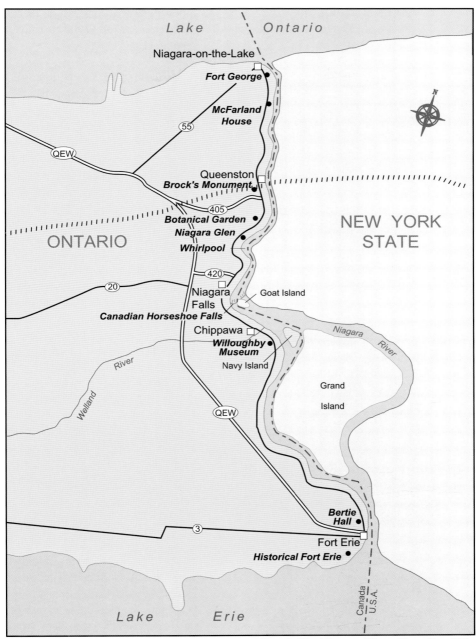

Map 4, The Niagara River, Canadian Side

place that captures your fancy.

The area including and immediately around Niagara Falls is described in Chapter 4.

The Reversible River

Since 1921, the Welland River has flowed in both directions. Normally flow is into the Niagara River. However, this situation is reversed and water flows upstream when it is drawn into a canal that feeds water to the Sir Adam Beck I power station.

We do not recommend any specific tour as you can drive/bike the entire parkway or select any segment of it. For example, the section between Niagara Falls and Niagara-on-the-Lake has a particularly large

Sentry at Fort Erie

NIAGARA PARKS COMMISSION

number of interesting features that are in close proximity and are convenient to visit.

Historic Fort Erie (\$) is a carefully restored military fort, which has a museum and is guarded by authentically dressed sentries. The first fort was built a little to the north of this site in 1764 as a defense against Indian attacks. The original fort and its successor were both destroyed by ice during winter storms that drove great masses of Lake Erie ice onto the shore. The present (third) fort was designed with four bastions connected by walls in the shape of a square to accommodate two to three hundred men. The fort saw considerable action during the War of 1812. Established by the British to guard the entrance to the Niagara River, it was captured by the Americans in the summer of 1814. Although the British could not recapture the fort, mounting setbacks elsewhere in the Niagara area caused the US commander to blow up the fort and withdraw to Buffalo. Shortly thereafter, the war ended. Restoration of the fort began in 1939.

Bertie Hall (\$), which now houses the Mildred Mahony Dollhouse Museum, was built in 1830 of stone and bricks hauled from Hamilton. It contains four black Italian marble fireplaces. Bertie Hall was used as a safe house in the Underground Railway that helped escaped slaves on their journey to freedom. The Hall was commandeered by Fenian soldiers during their seige of Fort Erie in 1866.

The Willoughby Museum is situated about 22 kilometres (14 miles) downriver from Fort Erie. Crammed into this small two-storey building are artifacts chronicling the settlement of Willoughby Township and the Chippawa area from the mid 1700s to the the late 1960s.

Navy Island, so named because a naval shipyard was established there in 1763, is located at the north end of Grand Island. The first ships to sail the upper Great Lakes under the British flag were built here. William Lyon Mackenzie encamped with his revolutionaries on the island in December 1837 and set up his short-lived Republic of Canada. After the burning of his supply ship, the Caroline, and heated sabre rattling between the US and British governments, the rebellion fizzled out. In the mid 1800s, the island was cleared for farming. In 1945, Navy Island was a candidate for the headquarters of the United Nations, but lost out to New York City. Today the island is a wild life preserve and is home to a herd of deer.

Kingsbridge Park and Chippawa (now a suburb of Niagara Falls) are at kilometre 28 (mile 17) just after crossing the Welland River. Father Hennepin, the first person to write about Niagara Falls, camped at this site in December, 1678. The first bridge, as well as government wharves, docks, and blockhouses for troops, were built here in about 1791. The blockhouse was the beginning of Fort Chippawa, also known as

Fort Welland, although no trace of it remains today. In the late 1700s and early 1800s, Chippawa was one of the larger communities in the Niagara area because it served as the southern terminus for portages around Niagara Falls. In addition, the Welland River, originally known as Chippawa Creek, was the exit of the first Welland Canal into the Niagara River. The road between Chippawa and Fort Erie served as a tow path with oxen pulling sailing ships up the river. After the second and subsequent Welland Canals by-passed Chippawa, the village declined in size and importance, and today there are no vestiges of the once busy port.

Kingsbridge Park has picnic facilities and a wading pool; the sand beach offers a cool swim.

Just past the park, note the International Control Works in the river and two high control gates that divert water through twin tunnels to the Sir Adam Beck Generating stations that are located further downstream.

Proceeding north, you soon approach Dufferin Islands and the Niagara Falls area. If you wish to read more about Niagara Falls, please refer to Chapter 4. If you wish to bypass the Falls and continue with the tour of the Parkway, please continue below.

Great Gorge Adventure (S) features a "Whitewater Boardwalk" that lets you stroll right next to the powerful, frothing rapids. The Rapids have fascinated sightseers since 1876, when a steam- powered incline railway took passengers to the river bank where a

Niagara Gorge rapids

stone walkway provided a close-up view of the surging rapids. The incline railway has been replaced by a high-speed elevator that will whisk you to the water's edge.

Niagara Spanish Aero Car (S) is located another kilometre (half mile) to the north. The Aero Car, suspended by six sturdy cables, has been carrying passengers directly over the Whirlpool Rapids since 1916. Its design and construction were supervised by a Spanish engineer, who modelled it after a similar aerocar in Spain.

Whirlpool Rapids can be seen from a few good vantage points along this section of the Parkway. From this safe height the rapids far below appear relatively calm. In actual fact, the waters attain speeds of 50 kilometres per hour (30 miles per hour) through this channel. Water travels counter-clockwise around the whirlpool, and the outgoing stream passes under-neath the incoming current to flow into the lower reaches of the river.

Needless to say, the Rapids have been the site of almost as many stunts as at the Falls, including tightrope walking, barrel riding, swimming, and even kayaking. Captain Matthew Webb, the first man to swim the English Channel, attempted to swim the Whirlpool Rapids in 1883. His body was not recovered for four days. Today, you can approach the Rapids in a jetboat from Niagara-on-the-Lake ($).

Whirlpool Golf Course ($), located another two kilometres (1.2 miles) further north, is open to the public. Ranked as one of Niagara's most beautiful courses, it features a large pond with hundreds of gold fish.

Niagara Glen Nature Reserve . The name Niagara Glen conjures up visions of a pleasant, peaceful glade. This image is reasonably accurate so

Wild Ride Through the Rapids
In 1860, the Maid of the Mist boat was purchased by a Montreal company – there was only one catch: the boat had to be delivered into Lake Ontario. After some deliberation, the captain and engineer volunteered to take the Maid through the Rapids. The huge waves tossed the boat like a leaf, tearing off the smoke stack and parts of the railings. But the plucky boat emerged from the rapids and sailed on to Lake Ontario and Montreal, where it worked for many years as a ferry.

long as you stay in the picnic area above the cliff. This grassed area, set amongst tall trees, was previously part of the river bed. In the mid 1850s, a saw mill operated on these flats, although no vestiges of it remain today.

But once you wander over the edge of the gorge, the scene changes

Niagara Spanish Aero Car

Pothole at Niagara Glen

dramatically, and a more apt descriptor would be the Devil's Half Acre or the Battleground of the Gods. Gigantic moss- covered boulders are strewn about in the most chaotic fashion, as though some superhuman powers had fought a pitched battle on this site, gouging rocks as large as houses from the ground and hurling them at each other. You can wander around this bizarre landscape along approximately 4 kilometres (2.5 miles) of trails, which can be accessed via a metal staircase down the initial, steepest part of the gorge. Rock climbers are often seen dangling precariously by ropes and pitons from the cliff face.

The trails lead down into the gorge, revealing the geologic strata that were laid down over four hundred million years ago. Although steep in places, the trails are well-marked and easily negotiated. The paths, which thread over, under, and around huge boulders that have been carved from the cliff face and were smoothed when Niagara Falls was here approximately eight thousand years ago, pass by various natural features including the mammoth pothole, the leaning rock, and the Devil's arch. The forest is primarily deciduous with maples, Staghorn sumacs, sassafras, tulip trees, and even some red mulberry trees. The ground cover is varied and includes poison ivy, so take care. This is one of our favourite walks because it is seldom crowded, and the scenery, with its tangle of giant boulders, has a surrealistic beauty.

Fishing has long been a favourite pastime at the Glen, and fishermen can often be seen casting their lines from the many rocks that are strewn along the shore. A word of caution: do not clamber onto these rocks as the water level can change suddenly and leave you stranded.

It is easy to spend an entire day at the Glen as it offers an excellent place to picnic and observe the geology and natural history of the Niagara gorge. A brochure that describes the paths and provides an insight into the geology, history of the gorge, and native vegetation is available in the Gift Shop or by calling/writing the Parks Commission (see Appendix). From late June to Labour Day, a park naturalist conducts free guided walks through the Glen. Contact the Parks Commission for times and topics to be covered. Sturdy hiking shoes are recommended.

Niagara Parks Botanical Gardens

The Botanical Gardens will be a highlight of this tour along the

Snake Kills Bridge

The lower banks of the Niagara Gorge with their numerous rock caverns and crevices were once a favourite haunt for the Timber Rattlesnake. Now feared to be extinct, they were very numerous and much feared in the early days. In 1906, the construction of a bridge at this point was cancelled because it was thought the snakes would cross the bridge and infest the US. The last reported siting of a Timber Ratlesnake was in 1959.

Parkway for anyone who loves flowers and gardening. The School of Horticulture, Canada's only residential school for training horticultural students, has been located here since

Hiking trail at Niagara Glen

Niagara Parks Botanical Gardens

Sir Adam Beck: Power Hungry

Adam Beck was a self-made man who gained his initial wealth by starting a cigar-box factory. He served as mayor of London, Ontario, before being elected to the provincial legislature in 1902. From the outset of his public life, he championed public power and was instrumental in establishing the provincial utility, Hydro-Electric Power Commission of Ontario, in 1906. He fought vigorously to get the first public hydro power plant built at Niagara Falls, which was later renamed in his honour. Beck passed away in 1925.

maintained gardens, such as the formal rose garden, the herb garden, the splendid arboretum, and the rock garden, which can be enjoyed through a self-guiding tour or simply by wandering through the floral kaleidoscope.

We love to come and stroll its many pathways, licking contentedly on ice cream cones, watching the many wedding parties that come to this beautiful locale for their wedding photos.

A new must-see attraction is the Butterfly Conservatory ($), the largest in North America, which houses over 2,000 free-flying butterflies in a lush tropical forest setting.

Sir Adam Beck Power Stations

About two kilometres (1.2 miles) further north are the two mighty hydroelectric power generating stations, Sir Adam Beck I and II. The former was completed in 1921 and was at that time the largest hydro power station in the world. The station is named after the first president of Ontario Hydro whose persistence and vision was responsible for its construction. Water is brought to this site via a canal from the Welland River near where it enters the Niagara River at Chippawa. The second power station was completed in 1954 and delivers water from above the Horseshoe Falls via large tunnels, which pass under the City of Niagara Falls. On the opposite bank of the Niagara Gorge is seen the large American power station Robert Moses. In total, the Niagara River generates about 4,400 megawatts of electricity.

1936. The diligence and artistry of hundreds of students over a period of more than six decades has created one of North America's most outstanding botanical gardens. It features over 40 hectares (100 acres) of immaculately

Together these mammoth stations, along with some smaller stations near the Falls, divert through their turbines a considerable quantity of water that would otherwise cascade over Niagara Falls. During peak viewing times, the flow of water over the Falls is about 2,832 cubic metres per second. At night time and during the non-tourist seasons about 50% of this flow is diverted through the power turbines. Thus, the face of the Falls changes depending on the time and season.

Unfortunately, no tours are given of the Canadian power plants. If you are interested in learning about such engineering wonders, the Robert Moses Power Station on the American side has an excellent reception centre and gives guided tours (see Chapter 6).

The Floral Clock
The Clock, located about 2.5 kilometres (1.5 miles) north of the Botanical Gardens is another free horticultural attraction. Built in 1950, the clock is one of the largest in the world at 12.2 metres (40 feet) in diameter; about 19,000 plants are used each year. The face of the clock is changed twice a season. Violas form a colourful centrepiece in early Spring, and in late May the clock is replanted with traditional carpet bedding plants. Westminster chimes and speakers intone the quarter hour and strike on the hour.

Adjacent to the Floral Clock is a lilac garden that contains over 1,200 mature plants representing over 225 varieties of lilac. Spread over four

Floral Deja Vu?
If you think the Floral Clock, one of Niagara's favourite photographic backdrops, looks familiar, perhaps it is. The Clock was fashioned after the famous floral clock built in 1903 in Princes St. Gardens in Edinburgh, Scotland.

hectares (ten acres), the lilacs bloom profusely in late May and June.

Queenston Heights Park
On summer weekends, this large picnic and recreation area perched on the edge of the Niagara Escarpment is packed with families enjoying the manicured lawns and majestic shade trees, band concerts at the band shell,

Brock's Monument

a children's wading pool (built in the 1812 earthwork redoubt of Fort Drummond), tennis courts, and a fine restaurant. You won't need a map to find this popular site – just head for the towering 50 metre (190 foot) Brock's monument.

The memorial commemorates Major General Sir Isaac Brock who died here in one of the fiercest battles of the War of 1812. The original monument was built in 1824, at which time Brock's remains were reinterred in the vault below the monument. Queenston Heights became a popular tourist destination, and for almost 100 years lake boats brought thousands of visitors from Toronto to this site. In 1840, the monument was blown up by one of the Mackenzie rebels. A new monument was completed in 1857, which has endured, with some repairs, until today.

A climb up the narrow spiralling stairs to the top of the monument will leave you breathless, both from the effort and the wonderful view across the southern Niagara farm land. It is this same escarpment edge where, about 12,000 years ago, the mighty cascades started to grind and wear away seemingly impenetrable rocks to form the 11-kilometre (6.8-mile) long Niagara Gorge.

A monument to Laura Secord, a cairn marking the southern end of the Bruce Trail, and various other historical markers are also found in the park.

A highly recommended walk is a self-guiding tour of the War of 1812 battlefield, which wends its way over the side of the escarpment down to the Village of Queenston. The stroll

evokes images of cannons crashing and muskets volleying as soldiers charged the entrenched high spots on Queenston Heights. It seems almost like fiction now as we gaze across the Niagara River at the pastoral landscape and the neighbouring United States of America, with whom Canada has so much in common, not the least of which is the world's longest undefended border.

The Battlefield Walk *(Map 5)*

The battlefield walk, which begins at Brock's monument, is illustrated by an excellent (free) brochure that is available from Park Canada staff and describes this walk and provides considerable detail about the War of 1812. If you cannot obtain a copy of the brochure, follow the abbreviated description provided below.

Walk east from Brock's Monument past the restaurant to the west side of Laura Secord's monument as shown on Map 5.

1. America declared war on Britain on June 18, 1812. The strategy was to attack Canada more or less simultaneously in four locations: near Detroit, Kingston, Montreal, and at Niagara. The attack on Niagara began at 3:00 am on October 13, 1812, as 600 Americans crossed the river in boats to attack the Village of Queenston. The British, however, were waiting for them and soon had

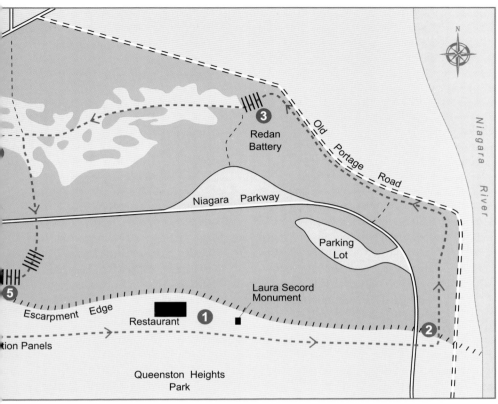

Map 5, The Battlefield Walk

the Americans pinned down on the beach. The night air was filled with the acrid smell of gunpowder as muskets and cannon roared.

2. Queenston was too well defended, so the attackers had to change their strategy. The American captain had heard of a small fishermen's path further upstream that led up the cliff, and at first light, a party of 60 soldiers trekked up the river and scaled the unguarded path.

3. When the American party reached the escarpment ridge, they spied a British artillery position with an 18-pounder cannon firing on their compatriots. The cannon was protected behind earthworks shaped like a half moon (redan) with General Isaac Brock directing operations. The Americans led a bayonet charge and quickly dislodged Brock and his men. With daylight emerging, Brock assembled 200 soldiers and led a charge to retake the redan. Not only did the counter-attack fail, but Brock was shot and killed. His aide-de-camp led another counter-attack, but this also failed to dislodge the Americans.

4. Earlier that morning, British reinforcements had marched from Fort George preceded by 100 Iroquois

Indians. The Indians had gained a reputation as fierce fighters and many American militia (volunteers) had refused to cross the river upon seeing the carnage at Queenston and hearing the Indian warriors.

5. By the middle of the afternoon, the reinforcements had arrived and were scaling the steep escarpment far enough west to be beyond the view of the Americans. At the top, they were joined by men from Fort Chippewa and a total of 1000 British soldiers advanced upon the American position. Outnumbered and holding the lower ground, the Americans soon surrendered.

6. The last stop is at a large panel due north of Brock's monument that provides an overview of the Battle of Queenston. Enjoy the wonderful panorama below. The Americans suffered a heavy toll. Not only were over 1200 men killed, wounded, or captured, but the loss showed the population of Upper Canada that they could repulse the American invasion.

A stone cairn at the east end of Queenston Heights marks the start of the Bruce Trail, the southern terminus of one of Canada's best known hiking trails (see Chapter 9 for a detailed description). We recommend that you walk westward along this trail for a little way to enjoy the woods, the limestone outcrops, and the view from the escarpment toward Lake Ontario and the rich fruitlands of Niagara-on-the-Lake. If you hunger for a longer stroll, then we recommend the Queenston Trails, which takes you further along the Bruce Trail and explores the historic Queenston Quarry (see Chapter 9, Tour 1).

Village of Queenston

Continue north along the Parkway, descending down the steep embankment of the Escarpment. At the bottom, take the second right and take a few moments to explore the historic Village of Queenston, one of the oldest settlements in the Niagara region. Like its counterpart across the river, Lewiston, it was an important port town when ships unloaded their cargos to be portaged around the Falls. In its heyday, Queenston must have been a lively spot. It is reported that the Village sported 13 taverns in the early 1800s; alas, not a single one remains today.

Although only a small village, Queenston boasts three museums that merit a visit. The first is the Laura Secord Homestead, the home where the War of 1812 heroine lived from 1803 to 1835 and from where she made her famous walk. The Mackenzie Heritage Printery is set in the restored home of William Lyon Mackenzie and features early printing, letterpress equipment, trades, and related crafts. It is here that Mackenzie issued his Colonial Advocate that criticized the Family Compact and called for an end to colonial rule by Britain. His efforts, including an aborted revolution against the Government, were instrumental in eventually bringing independent self-government to Canada. The Samuel E. Weir collection, funded by a private endowment, features historical

Canadian, American and European art, antiques and a reference library set in a picturesque house next to the river.

Queenston is renowned amongst birdwatchers as one of the best places in Canada to see gulls. Up to 13 species visit Queenston on their fall migration southward including Bonaparte's gull, the herring gull, the rarer European little gull, the black-headed Sabene's gull, the Ireland and glaucous gulls. The best spot to view the birds is from the docks.

Continuing north, note the many grand homes and large shade trees. The Inniskillin and Reif wineries (see Chapter 11) make pleasant stops on this journey.

McFarland House and Park are located on the right hand side at kilo-metre 55 (mile 34). Guides in period costume will show you this gracious red brick Georgian house built in 1800. Home baking and tea are served. The park is a pleasant place for a leisurely picnic, perhaps enjoying a chilled white wine from one of the wineries. The park is divided by a deep ravine, from the foot of which British forces crossed the river in the War of 1812 and cap-tured Fort Niagara.

Another kilometre (half mile) down the Parkway and you are entering the outskirts of the pic-turesque and historic Town of Nia-gara-on-the-Lake, which is described in Chapter 12.

An ambitious Grand Tour of Nia-gara, which includes the Niagara Parkway as well as the Welland Canal and more, is presented in Chapter 14 (Tour 6).

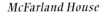

McFarland House

Chapter 6

FOLLOW THE NIAGARA RIVER:
THE AMERICAN SIDE

Old Fort Niagara

Whereas the Canadian side of the Niagara River is almost one continuous strip of parkland, the American side is an interesting mixture of industrial development and parkland. But before you turn your nose up at the thought of factories with belching smoke stacks, you should realize that the industries have their own historical fascination and have stemmed largely from the availability of cheap hydro-electric power from Niagara Falls. Furthermore, there are many spots along the River that are beautiful, and a tour along the river is rewarding, particularly the stretch between Niagara Falls and Lake Ontario.

We describe the American Niagara River from Buffalo at the southern end to Fort Niagara at the northern mouth of the river at Lake Ontario. You may choose to explore all or only a segment of this area. For example, a pleasant outing is to explore Lewiston and Fort Niagara (see Map 6).

Buffalo

Buffalo, with a population of about 320,000 and serving a much larger urban and rural area, is the largest city in western New York State and the commercial giant of the Niagara region. Buffalo may have remained an obscure village if it were

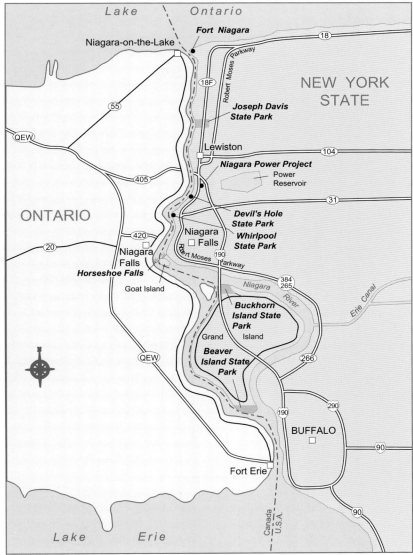

Map 6, The Niagara River, American Side

not for the construction of the Erie
Canal, which transformed it into a
booming port. Grain elevators punctuated its skyline, and its stockyards
were second only to Chicago's. But
Buffalo also gained notoriety. In

1901, the city hosted the Pan-Amer-
ican Exposition, where President
McKinley was assassinated.

Since Buffalo is a major metro-
politan centre with a rich cultural
heritage and a wide spectrum of

attractions, it is not described in detail. However, some areas and attractions worth seeing are summarized here.

Albright-Knox Art Gallery at 1285 Elmwood Avenue is considered one of the nation's finest museums for modern art.

Buffalo and Erie County Botanical Gardens at 2655 South Park Avenue at McKinley Parkway consist of 4.4 hectares (11 acres) of gardens and feature a Victorian-style conservatory built in the 1890s.

Buffalo and Erie County Naval and Servicemen's Park at One Naval Park Cove on the waterfront is the largest inland naval park of its kind in the country and includes a guided-missile cruiser and a submarine.

Buffalo Museum of Science at 1020 Humboldt Parkway includes many fascinating and educational exhibits of science as well as a 106 hectare (264 acre) nature preserve.

Buffalo Zoological Gardens at 300 Parkside Avenue at Delaware Park is home to more than 1,000 animals including the rare Indian rhinoceros and the white tiger.

Frank Lloyd Wright (1867-1959)
Wright is considered the creative genius of American architecture, and was also a prolific writer. His works were dominated by a profound sense of principle, and he was a pioneer of modern technology in commercial architecture.

Tifft Nature Preserve at 1200 Fuhrmann Boulevard is part of the Buffalo Museum of Science and features a 30 hectare (75 acre) cattail marsh and eight kilometres (five miles) of nature trails. Self-guided walks and a variety of nature programs are offered.

Theodore Roosevelt Inaugural National Historic Site at 641 Delaware Avenue is one of the few inaugural sites located outside Washington, D.C. On August 14, 1901, Theodore Roosevelt was inaugurated as the 26th president in the library of the Wilcox Mansion.

Architecture! Buffalo was a thriving hub of transportation and industry at the turn of the 20th century, and its glorious past is exemplified in its wonderful architecture. Our Lady of Victory Basilica and National Shrine rivals some of Europe's finest cathedrals. Buffalo has five homes designed by Frank Lloyd Wright and extensive parks designed by Frederick Law Olmstead. Olmstead was a brilliant landscape architect who designed a number of outstanding parks, including Central Park in New York City. A copy of "Buffalo Architecture: A Guide" can be ordered from the Buffalo Convention and Visitors Bureau (see Appendix).

Proceeding north from Buffalo along Interstate 190, a high-level bridge crosses the Niagara River bringing you onto Grand Island (see Map 6).

Grand Island
Grand Island, surrounded by the waters of Niagara River, is a pleasant island to explore by bicycle or by car. The island was once covered by a forest of white oak, which sheltered a large population of deer and was a

favorite Indian hunting ground. It features an amusement park, Martin's Fantasy Island, and two state parks. Buckhorn Island State Park at the north end of the island is a nature preserve and has no amenities. It is a wonderful place for peaceful nature hikes. Beaver Island State Park at the southern end of the island is a beehive of activity in the summer with an 18-hole golf course, beach, and numerous picnic areas. It also features a sledding hill during the winter months.

Proceed north on Interstate 190 and exit onto the Robert Moses Parkway as soon as you have crossed the Niagara River. Travel along the edge of the Niagara River into Niagara Falls (see Chapter 4 for a description of the Falls).

Between Buffalo and Niagara Falls you will notice a number of chemical industries. Created to tap the power of the River, these and other factories have, unfortunately, made their own impact on the river through pollution that seeps from numerous landfills.

Just before entering the City of Niagara Falls, note the two tall structures at the river's edge. They are large gates controlling water intake into two tunnels that carry water to the Robert Moses power project, which you will see further downstream. Plaques mark the site of the former Fort Shlosser, built in 1759 by the British.

On leaving Niagara Falls, travel north along the Robert Moses Parkway.

Whirlpool State Park

This small state park is located on the Robert Moses State Parkway a few miles north of Niagara Falls. Overlooking the Niagara gorge, the park has a self-guiding trail that explains the geology of Niagara Falls. There are excellent overviews of the whirlpool rapids in the Niagara River, and far below you might see the jet boat fighting against the strong currents.

Devil's Hole State Park

It is hard to imagine that this quiet place was the scene of a bloody massacre over two hundred years ago. In the 1700s, Lewiston and Queenston were busy port towns. As no Welland Canal existed, ships brought their goods to Lewiston where they were off-loaded and transported via a portage around Niagara Falls. For many years, the Seneca Indians had earned a livelihood by carrying trade goods over the portage. The introduction of wagons, however, deprived them of their main source of income and was a major disruption to their way of life. This massacre was in retaliation to the loss of their jobs and could be considered one of the first incidents of labour violence in Niagara.

On September 14, 1763, a wagon train was rumbling past this spot when 500 Seneca Indians leapt from the bushes with blood curdling shrieks. Soon, all the victims and their belongs had been hurdled over the gorge, leaving the forest quiet and peaceful. The shots had been heard at Lewiston, and a detachment of soldiers was sent to investigate. As the troop reached the quiet glade, the carnage was re-enacted leaving only two survivors. Over a hundred people died, and a nearby stream is called Bloody Run in memory of that horrible day.

Niagara Power Project Visitor's Centre

Located about eight kilometres (five miles) north of Niagara Falls on Lewiston Road is one of the largest hydroelectric power projects in the world. The project is comprised of two components: The Robert Moses Niagara Power Plant and the Lewiston Pump-Generating station. Together they have a capacity of 2,400 megawatts. Water is brought to the site from above Niagara Falls by two large underground tunnels, which pass under the City of Niagara Falls, NY.

The station was built from 1958 to 1961 on a rush basis, to make up for the power shortage caused by the destruction of the two Schoellkopf generating stations in 1956. It has 13 generator-turbines and on its completion was the largest hydroelectric plant in the world. The plant is named after Robert Moses, the chairman of the New York Power Authority during the construction.

Additional power is supplied from the 760-hectare (1900-acre) reservoir to the east of the power plant, which is like a storage battery. During the night, when electricity demand is low, the reservoir is filled by 12 reversible pumps. During the day, when electricity demand is higher and less water can be diverted

from the river, the water is released and flows through the reversible pumps that act as generators and create electricity.

The New York Power Authority has developed an excellent visitors centre called Power Vista, which is bright and spacious, has excellent displays, and offers wonderful panoramas of the Niagara gorge and river. You can tour the history of electricity, see exciting exhibits, and operate hands-on displays. A fishing platform at the river's edge provides an opportunity to catch salmon, trout, and steelhead.

Tours of the facility can also be arranged by calling the New York Power Authority (see Appendix).

Lewiston

Nestled on the banks of the Niagara River below the escarpment, Lewiston has a Norman Rockwell-like charm and ambience as well as considerable historical significance. As the northern terminus of the portage around Niagara Falls, it was a bustling port in the late 1700s and early 1800s. It is hard to imagine that in its heyday Lewiston had a population of 6,000 while Buffalo consisted of only a few cabins.

The Village of Lewiston has a designated historical district consisting of six blocks of beautiful homes, churches, and a museum, most of which were built prior to 1850. Lewiston has many parallels with Niagara-on-the-Lake. Both towns were razed during the War of 1812, both are quaint and picturesque towns with a large number of stately, historic mansions. And both towns have turned to the arts as their main focus with Art Park in Lewiston and the Shaw Festival in Niagara-on-the-Lake drawing thousands of visitors each year.

Some places worth a visit include:
The Lewiston Museum at 469 Plain Street is a white clapboard former church built circa 1835.

The Frontier House on Centre Street was built in 1824 and has served as an inn ever since. At one time it was known as the finest hotel west of Albany. Dignitaries who have visited here include Governor DeWitt Clinton, Edward, Prince of Wales, Washington Irving, President McKinley, and Charles Dickens.

The First Presbyterian Church

Fence at Barton House

Hennepin Hall

The First Presbyterian Church on Cayuga Street. Established in 1817, the site also has a monument honouring the Underground Railway.

The Barton House at 210 3rd Street on the corner with Center Street. This house was rebuilt in 1815 after the original was destroyed by the British in 1813. The hill on which the house is built was the site of an artillery position during the Battle of Queenston.

An historic inn is located at 650 Center Street close to the river. Built circa 1840, it still operates as an inn and has wonderful views onto the Niagara River from its deck.

Hennepin Hall at 620 Center Street is a stately two-story house. Constructed circa 1833, it was the home of many prominent Lewiston residents. In 1953, it was purchased by the Catholic parish and is now the rectory.

Artpark, a 80 hectare (200-acre) centre for live entertainment and the arts, is the main focus of Lewiston. A covered theatre with adjoining outside lawn seating offers musicals, dance, classical, pop, and jazz concerts. Artpark also presents various arts and crafts workshops and exhibits. The grounds themselves are of considerable historical interest and contain the Hotchkiss stone quarry, the site at which mastodon bones were found, and the site of a Neuter Indian camp called Ongiara, which was visited by Champlain in 1615, from which the name Niagara has derived.

A delightful way to spend an afternoon is to explore the old houses of Lewiston, followed by a picnic on the grounds of Artpark overlooking the Niagara River, and then to listen to a jazz concert, while relaxing on a blanket on the lawn with a bottle of wine.

Travelling north from Lewiston along Highway 18F, you soon encounter *Joseph Davis State Park*, which is a pleasant place for a picnic and features an 18-hole frisbee course and a dock for boating and fishing.

Old Fort Niagara

Constructed in 1726 to guard the entrance to the Niagara River and the upper lakes, Old Fort Niagara is the oldest building in the Great Lakes area. The strategic significance of this location was recognized as early as 1678 when the French explorer LaSalle built Fort Conti here to protect the fur trade. In 1726, the present fort was constructed, but to allay the concerns of the Indians, the French made the fort to resemble a French chateau. However, the thick stone walls with openings for cannons indicate the true military intention of this structure. The French and Indian wars led to Fort Niagara being captured by the English in 1759. In 1796, the fort again changed hands as it became part of the new United States of America.

The fort played a key role in the War of 1812, twice serving as the launching point for successful invasions of Canada. Toward the end of the War, Fort Niagara was captured by the British, only to be returned to the USA when hostilities ceased.

The fort's original stone buildings have been preserved as they stood before the American Revolution, including massive stone walls and bastions, dozens of cannons, a moat and drawbridge, blockhouses, stockade, and more. Although it is open year round, the best time to visit is from July 1 until Labour Day, when the Old Fort Niagara Guard fire muskets and cannons in exciting drills and reenactments.

The fort is located adjacent to the Fort Niagara State Park, which includes a lighthouse, an 1812 cemetery, and other park amenities.

More Information

A detailed brochure, *"Welcome to your Niagara Historic Trail,"* describing the tour along the Niagara River (as well as along Lake Ontario and the Erie Canal) is available from Niagara County Tourism (see Appendix).

Chapter 7

WELLAND CANAL: STAIRCASE FOR GIANT SHIPS

Welland Canal: Looking north at Lock 3

The first impression of a modern lake-faring freighter is of its overwhelming size. It doesn't seem possible that something of such immense proportions could even be built, much less be able to dock, load, and sail the lakes. Yet dozens of lakers and "salties" (sea-going ships) ply up and down the Welland Canal every day, casting enormous shadows as they cruise incongruously past lush orchards and vineyards.

Longer than two football fields and weighing more than 30,000 tonnes, how is it possible to lift these behemoths up and over the cliff face of the Niagara escarpment? Not only is this done on a routine basis, but the technology is so simple that ships have been routinely hoisted up and down the escarpment for over 150 years.

Engineers discovered the trick long ago – let gravity and water do the work. The locks are filled and emptied by water flowing downhill from Lake Erie toward Lake Ontario. Many fascinating hours can be spent watching how the gates are opened and shut to control the water flow, allowing ponderous monsters from all corners of the world to sail into the middle of the North American continent.

Originally constructed in 1829 to link Lake Erie with Lake Ontario and offer ships a safe detour around Niagara Falls, the Welland Canal has a long and colourful history, which can be explored in a number of tours by car, by bicycle or on foot.

The first Welland Canal started from Port Dalhousie and followed Martindale Pond (Twelve Mile Creek) and then Dick's Creek to Thorold. The first Canal used a total of 40 wooden locks. Before long, the Canal and its locks proved to be too small for the growing size of ships. To rectify the situation, the second Canal, which followed the route of the first Canal, was constructed from 1842 to 1845. This Canal was wider than the first and had a total of 27 stone locks. The third Canal, constructed in 1870, saw a further widening as well as a realignment of the northern end, away from Twelve Mile and Dick's Creek (see Map 9).

The current (fourth) canal, completed in 1932, uses only eight locks and follows a nearly direct north-south route from St. Catharines in the north to Port Colborne in the south. The canal has had a profound influence on the Niagara area, creating new communities along the line of the waterway and encouraging industrial development and regional expansion.

The canal forms part of the St. Lawrence Seaway, which allows cargo transportation between the Atlantic Ocean and the upper Great Lakes and has been a major factor in the opening up and development of the interior of the continent. Bulk goods

William Hamilton Merritt: The Father of the Canal

Born in the USA in 1793, Merritt and his family came to Upper Canada as Loyalists in 1796 and settled in St. Catharines. After serving in the War of 1812, Merritt became a successful merchant and mill-owner. He was the main force and visionary behind the first Welland Canal, which was completed under the direction of the private Welland Canal Company, rather than by the government. Merritt was elected to the Upper Canada legislature and served from 1832-1841; he was elected to the Legislative Assembly of Canada and served from 1841 to 1860. He passed away in 1862.

in prodigious quantities pass up and down the Niagara Escarpment. For example, in 1995, eight hundred salties and 2,500 lakers passed through the canal. The three most significant cargoes were grain, iron ore, and coal.

The impact that this stretch of engineered water has had on the economy can not be understated, and it may even be argued that the Canal has been the saviour of Canada. It promoted the union of Lower and Upper Canada and was a major force in preventing the commercial takeover of the country by the

Canal Facts

Number of locks	8
Total lift	99.5 m (326 feet)
Lift locks	Locks 1 to 7
Water control lock	Lock 8
Flight locks that climb the escarpment	Locks 4, 5, and 6
Lock width	24 m (79 feet)
Lock length	262 m (860 feet)
Time for a ship to traverse the canal	11 hours

Americans after their Erie Canal opened in 1825.

The Welland Canal, which is approximately 32 kilometres (20 miles) long, is only surpassed in length by the Suez and Panama Canals. However, the Welland Canal has the highest lift and was the first to be built.

Although the Welland Canal is a major transportation corridor for ships, it poses an obstacle to east-west car and rail travel. Engineers have come up with a variety of different solutions ranging from the graceful, towering Garden City Skyway, which carries traffic high over the tallest ships, to the three tunnels that burrow under the Canal. In addition, there are 10 rail or road bridges that must lift or swing or fold out of the way every time a ship passes by. Travellers who are caught in the lineups that form when a bridge is "up" watch in frustrated fascination as a colossal ship slowly steams past.

TOUR 1:
Introduction to the Canal

If you only have time for one canal stop, the Lock 3 Viewing Complex and Museum is the place to go. The complex houses a tourist information and interpretive centre complete with ship schedules, the St.Catharines Historical Museum, the Ontario Lacrosse Hall of Fame, a restaurant, picnic areas, and free parking. Be sure to climb the special viewing platform where you can look down onto the decks of gigantic ships as they ponderously manoeuvre

through the lock with only inches to spare. You will hear languages from across the globe and watch as steel hawsers, the thickness of your arm, are attached to stanchions beside the lock. Watching the ponderous progress of the ships, which contrasts starkly to the hustle bustle of our modern time-conscious lives, is pleasantly soothing.

The Canal forms the main theme at the St. Catharines Historical Museum. An extensive display of canal memorabilia is presented, which provides a fascinating insight into the days of the early canals. The exhibits include photographs and models illustrating the early canals, towpaths, three-masted schooners, shipbuilding yards, and stonemasons from Scotland who crafted large limestone blocks into locks that stand, virtually indestructible, even a century later. Don't miss the computerized working scale model of Lock 3.

Ship schedules for the day are posted at the interpretive centre, along with information on the ships' nationalities, sizes, destinations, and cargoes.

TOUR 2:
Welland Canal Recreation Trail

Constructed in 1995, this nine-kilometre (5.6 mile) recreation trail, which stretches along the west side of the canal between Glendale Avenue at the south end and Lakeshore Road at the north end, has become one of the most popular places in St. Catharines for walkers, joggers, bikers, and roller bladers. Occasional park benches allow a quiet rest and the opportunity to watch massive ships passing by and to muse about their cargoes and their destinations.

The trail can be accessed at many points along its length; however, a good starting point is the Lock 3 Viewing Complex, which has ample parking.

The immense popularity of this recreation trail has provided an impetus to the long-overdue plan to extend the trail along the entire length of the Canal. Hopefully, this plan will reach fruition in the near future.

TOUR 3:
The Entire Canal by Car (Map 7)

Although roads do not parallel the canal the entire way, the Canal can be accessed at many locations, allowing for a rewarding driving tour. Allow time for driving at least 50 kilometres (31 miles) with numerous stops. We suggest that you start at the northern end, which is the most accessible. Government Road lies on the western side of the canal and extends from Lakeshore Road near Lake Ontario to Lock 7 in Thorold. This is a pleasant drive with views of lock 1 and Port Weller Dry Docks and then lock 2 at Carlton Street. As you pass under the Garden City Skyway, built in 1963 and carrying the heavy traffic of the Queen Elizabeth Highway over the canal, note the older Homer Bridge, the site of colossal traffic jams in the days before the Skyway. There are park benches along the way with many spots to stop for a closer look at the passing ships or for watching the many walkers and roller-bladers on the recreational trail. Next you pass the Lock 3 viewing complex, described in Tour 1

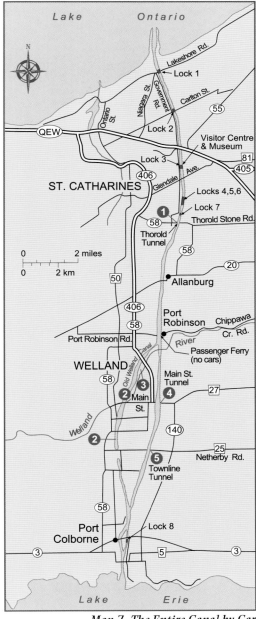

Map 7, The Entire Canal by Car

and well worth a visit.

The lift bridge at Glendale Avenue is our favorite with its twin latticed

Ship in Lock 5

towers and the bridge operator's house that forms part of the bridge structure and rides up and down every time a ship passes. This is no job for someone with a fear of heights!

Continue southward along Government Road to the flight locks (4,5,6). This is an excellent place for ship watchers, as these locks have been twinned to allow ships to simultaneously travel both up and down the escarpment. It is a remarkable sight to see six adjacent locks, often containing two or more giant ships travelling in opposite directions.

Continue along Government Road heading south for a few hundred metres until you reach Lock 7, the last lift to the top of the escarpment. Looking back you have a grand view of the canal, the skyway, and Lake Ontario. On a clear, crisp day, the CN Tower and skyscrapers of Toronto can be seen shimmering on the horizon.

Government Road ends here, and you must now swing away from the canal. Access to the Welland Canal by car further to the south is only gained by roads that are perpendicular to the canal and short stretches of parallel service roads maintained by the St. Lawrence Seaway Authority.

Turn left (south) onto Chapel Street and follow it as it curves around to Ormond Street. Turn left and follow Ormond as it curves to the west and turn left on Pine Street. Cross over the Highway 58 overpass and immediately turn left onto the ramp and join Highway 58 as it goes east under the Welland Canal. From this point on, meander southward toward Port Colborne using Map 7 as a guide.

Points of interest along the canal that are south of Lock 7 include the following:

1. Highway 58 passes under the Welland Canal via the Thorold Tunnel. Constructed in 1968, it was the first of three tunnels that pass under the canal.

2. Welland Recreational Waterway. In 1973, work to re-route the Welland Canal around the City of Welland was completed. The section of the canal that is no longer used for shipping now provides recreation in the form of water skiing, boating, rowing, and other leisure activities.

3. Merritt Island is the strip of land between the Welland River and the old canal (the Welland Recreational Waterway). The island features picnic facilities, hiking, biking, cross-country ski trails, and a Welland Canal historic marker.

4. The Main Street tunnel in Welland carries Main Street traffic under the canal. This tunnel was completed in 1972.

5. The Townline Tunnel in south Welland, completed in 1973, carries both car and train traffic under the canal.

Port Colborne, the southern terminus of the Welland Canal, is well worth a visit.

Lock 8 is located in Fountainview Park, where an elevated observation deck allows a view of one of the world's longest locks. The Port Colborne Historical & Marine Museum at 280 King Street features over 10,000 artifacts as well as an original schoolhouse and blacksmith shop. You can dig your toes into sand and cool down with a swim at Nickel Beach.

An ambitious Grand Tour of Niagara, which includes the Welland Canal as well as the Niagara Parkway and more, is presented in Chapter 14 (Tour 6).

TOUR 4:
The Entire Canal by Bicycle:
The Merritt Trail (Map 8)

The Merritt Trail, developed by the Welland Canal Preservation Society, is a 45 kilometre (28 mile) hiking/biking trail that crosses the Niagara Peninsula from Lake Ontario to Lake Erie following the routes of past and present Welland Canals. This is an excellent way to see the Canal because almost the entire route is along the banks of the Canal. Note

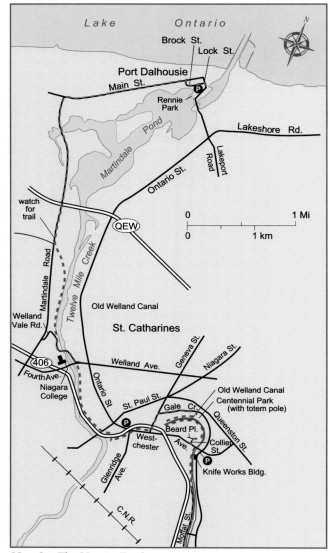

Map 8a, The Merritt Trail

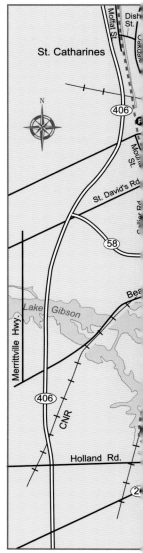

Map 8b, The Merritt Trai

that a mountain bike is recommended as this is an off-road trail that can be quite rough in places. You should allow all day for this tour, and will need to make arrangements to get picked up at the finish.

At the northern end between Lake

Ontario and Thorold, we offer an alternative path in addition to the original path.

See Maps 8a, 8b, 8c, and 8d for the route of the Merritt Trail. Note that the Trail is identified by yellow paint blazes (2 inches wide by 5

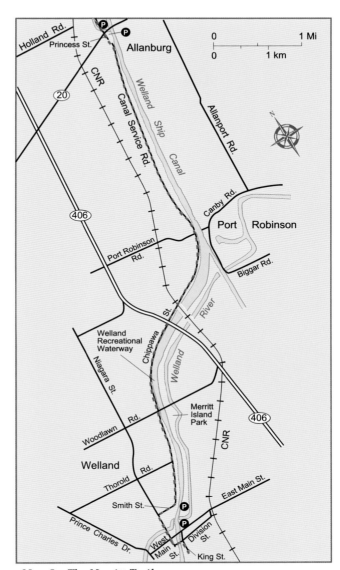

Map 8c, The Merritt Trail

inches high) in a similar fashion as the Bruce Trail, that is, a single blaze indicates the trail continues in the same direction, whereas two blazes indicate the trail will change direction, with the top blaze offset in the direction of the turn.

We must offer a word of caution. As with the Bruce Trail, the Merritt Trail can be confusing in places, so be sure to maintain contact with the yellow blazes.

Begin the tour at either the Rennie Park or the Lakeside Park

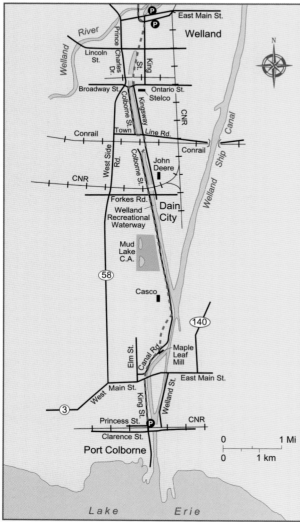

Map 8d, The Merritt Trail

parking lot at the end of Lakeport Road in Port Dalhousie. Join Main Street and proceed west to Martindale Road. Turn left and proceed south crossing the Queen Elizabeth Highway. About 0.5 kilometres (0.3 miles) past the QEW, opposite Erion Road, take a gravel path on the left (east) side of the road that angles down into the Twelve Mile Creek valley. Follow the path until it joins Welland Vale Road. Turn left, cross the Creek, and look to the right for the continuation of the path. Continue along the path. As you come off the ramp after crossing the 406 Highway on a narrow pedestrian/bicycle bridge, make sure to turn sharply left, rather than continuing straight. Follow the path to where it ends by Geneva Street. Proceed north along Geneva Street crossing Highway 406 and turn right on Gale Crescent. Watch for steps leading down to Centennial Park, proceed west until you get to the south side of the Creek; then continue in an easterly direction following Dick's Creek. Cross Westchester Avenue, and the path resumes on the right side of the Creek.

Continue along the path, crossing a set of train tracks and Glendale Avenue. Across Glendale, the path climbs the escarpment beside the won-

Canal Pilots

Manoeuvring a ship that is over 213 metres (700 feet) long through the narrow locks of the Welland Canal is quite a challenge. To assist a ship's captain, a pilot is taken aboard for the passage and becomes the ship's navigator. You can tell that a pilot is aboard by the white and red flag that the ship flies.

derful stone locks that comprise the Neptune's Staircase of the second Welland Canal.

At the top, proceed south following Bradley Street which turns into John Street. A slight jog to the east takes you onto Front Street, Thorold; follow it and then go through the Battle of Beaverdams Park. Pick up Ormond Street, on your left, and follow it as it curves to the west. At Pine Street turn left. Cross Highway 58 and turn left following the yellow blazes to Patricia Street. Proceed south along the marked trails as shown on Maps 8b to 8d.

Alternative Beginning

It is shorter and simpler if you start at Lock 1 at the intersection of Government Road and Lakeshore Road, St. Catharines. Follow the Welland Canal recreational path south (see Tour 2) to its end at Glendale Avenue.

Continue by heading south along Government Road to its end on Chapel Street just past Lock 7. Turn left (south) on Chapel Street and follow it as it curves around to Ormond Street. Turn left and follow Ormond as it curves to the west and turn left on Pine Street. Cross over the Highway 58 overpass and turn left following the yellow blazes to Patricia Street.

Proceed south along the marked trails as shown on Maps 8b to 8d.

The rest of the Merritt Trail is fairly straightforward. But be sure to keep in contact with the yellow blazes.

TOUR 5:
History of the Canal (Map 9)

This 28 kilometre (17 mile) tour of the northern end of the Canal provides an overview of the history of the Welland Canal and can be enjoyed by car or by bicycle. If driving, allow two to four hours. Although a tour by bicycle will be relatively strenuous and will take a full day, it will offer a closer look at the many interesting features of this tour. Refer to Map 9 for the stops described below.

1. Lock 3 Viewing Area. This is the starting point and is described in Tour 1.

2. Lock 2 at Carlton Street. Although canals typically require that a ditch be dug, along this stretch the canal takes on the unusual form of being raised above ground level and is contained between water-tight embankments. This is because the land surface here slopes downward toward Lake Ontario whereas the stretch of canal between locks must be kept level.

3. Lock 1. Port Weller Drydocks can be seen across the Canal. Since 1946, the Drydocks have built and repaired numerous lake and ocean-going vessels. Note the bridge at the lock, a single-leaf rolling lift bascule bridge which carries both car and rail traffic. A weir is located to the east of Lock 1, which controls the height of water in the Canal by discharging surplus water through its sluices. Each lock on the Canal has such an accompanying weir.

4. Continue northwards along the west side of the Canal. Two long breakwaters extend the Canal for 2.4

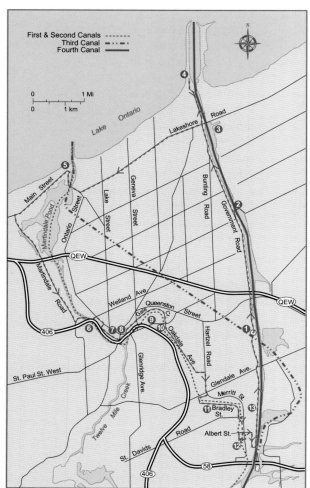

First & Second Canals --------
Third Canal ---·---·---
Fourth Canal ━━━

Map 9, History of the Canal

5. Return to Lakeshore Road and proceed west to Port Dalhousie. After crossing the bridge, turn right at Murphy's Restaurant and park at Lakeside Park. Port Dalhousie was the northern entrance to the first three canals and became the focus for industrial and commercial activity. For example, a rail line was opened between Port Colborne and Port Dalhousie in 1859, which lightened downbound ships by unloading them at Port Colborne and reloading them at Port Dalhousie. In 1901, Lakeside Park was a thriving amusement park with tourists coming from Toronto by excursion boat and from St. Catharines by streetcar. The memory of this historic tourist boom still echoes in the 5-cent carousel, which is a popular stop for children today.

Map 9 shows the routes of the first three canals through Port Dalhousie. Only Lock 1 of the second canal, constructed of large limestone blocks, still remains today, opposite Murphy's Restaurant. A wrought-iron barrier fence displays the four stages of Canal evolution. In 1987 turbines for generating electricity were installed near the previous location of Lock 1 of the third canal. This development, which supplies about 3% of St. Catharines' energy demand, reflects the ongoing use of the Canal as a source of power as well as transportation. The former

kilometres (1.5 miles) into Lake Ontario to protect its entrance from wind, currents, and siltation. A lighthouse is located on the western breakwater, and a small harbour is nestled within the two breakwaters on the eastern side. You will likely see one or more ships lying at anchor in the lake awaiting entry to the Canal. This is an excellent vantage point to enjoy a sunset.

Lock 2 of the third Canal is located on the east side of Martindale Pond and is accessible from Jaycee Gardens on Ontario Street.

The port remained open to commercial vessels until the 1960s even though the entrance to the fourth canal was moved to Port Weller in 1932. Recent years have seen the transition of this area to an attractive tourist locale featuring boutiques, taverns, a marina, the carousel, and walks along the beach and western pier. A walking tour of Port Dalhousie is described in Chapter 13.

6. Leave Port Dalhousie by driving west along Main Street. Turn left on Martindale Road and follow the west bank of Twelve Mile Creek, the former course of the first and second Canals. Good views are available of Martindale Pond, which has been transformed from a busy harbour for steam ships to a world class rowing course. About 2.1 kilometres (1.3 miles) south of the Queen Elizabeth Highway, turn left on Welland Vale Road, which drops into the valley bottom, and stop at Niagara College. The curving, narrow ditch on the west side of the Creek is the only surviving remnant of the First Canal. The second Canal cut across the bend in a straight line and the remains of Lock 2 may be seen at this spot. St. Catharines was a popular spa resort in the latter 1800s, and ships bearing visitors from Toronto disembarked near this point. The passengers enjoyed salt and mineral springs as well as band concerts in nearby Montebello Park.

The grist and saw mill of William Hamilton Merritt, the founder of the Welland Canal, was located at the south end of Welland Vale, although no vestige of it remains today.

Sailing ships in Port Dalhousie Harbour, circa 1878

ST. CATHARINES HISTORICAL MUSEUM, N1014

7. Yates Street. Proceed east on Welland Vale. Turn left on Welland Avenue and immediately right on Ontario Street and right again at Adams Street. The lands of Montebello Park were owned by Merritt and were purchased by the City in 1887. Turn left on Yates Street, one of the prettiest in St. Catharines with its regal mansions reflecting former days of economic glory, and stop near St. Paul Street overlooking the valley. A plaque honours Louis Shickluna, whose shipyards occupied the valley below. The shipyards produced over 200 ships between 1840 and 1880 and were renowned as the largest in Canada. Although little remains today, this part of the valley was heavily industrialized in the 1800s and included a wheel factory, a knife works, and a brewery.

Walk south onto the south side of Burgoyne Bridge, which offers a sweeping panorama of Twelve Mile Creek with Dick's Creek, the former first and second Canal route, entering from the east. Numerous industries were located on the north side of the former canals and were supplied with power from a hydraulic raceway. The colour of the water in Dick's Creek is graphic evidence of continuing pollution from industry along this canal valley – industry that originated as a direct result of the Canals. The prominent building at the corner of St. Paul and Yates Streets, which now houses the CKTB radio station, is the former home of William Hamilton Merritt.

8. As the entrance to St. Paul Street has been blocked off, retrace your route to Ontario Street, turn right, and turn right again at St. Paul Street. Turn immediately left on McGuire Street and drive into Canal Valley, stopping near the Canada Hair Cloth Mill. The Canal transformed St. Catharines from an agricultural village to an industrial town, with twelve mills operating on the raceway by 1847. The raceway remained in operation until 1929. This part of Dick's Creek was placed underground to hide the contaminated waters and allow construction of Highway 406, which now carries automobile traffic where ships once travelled.

9. Proceed east along McGuire, turning left at the stop lights (Geneva Street) and immediately right at Gale Crescent. This curving street follows the infilled former raceway. The hospital on the left was founded in 1865 and was originally named the St. Catharines General and Marine Hospital, reflecting the importance of the Canal. Stop at the plaque commemorating William Pierpoint, after whom Dick's Creek is named. Pierpoint was an American slave who came to Canada in 1780 and was granted land in this vicinity. Centennial Gardens occupies the valley bottom, replete with a large Haida Indian totem pole.

10. Proceeding approximately southeast along Oakdale Avenue, the Canal Valley contains a number of charming stone locks of the second Canal. The second Canal was built to the west and slightly higher than the first Canal to allow the latter to remain operational during the construction period. Each lock attracted a

Lift bridge at Glendale Avenue, St. Catharines

mill or factory. The Merritt Trail, which follows the Canal Valley along its west side, can be accessed from a parking lot on the south side of Westchester Street, just to the west of Oakdale Avenue. A walk southwards along this pleasant curving trail is recommended as it features several stone locks, still in excellent condition after more than a century, in a peaceful tree-lined setting, marred only by the polluted water in the creek.

11. Neptune's Staircase. Proceed along Oakdale Avenue until it ends at Hartzel Road. Turn right and right again at Glendale Avenue. Note both the current and historic industries. Turn left at Mountain Street and immediately left again at Bradley Street. Park about half way up the hill. This site forms the highlight of the tour and is well worth a visit on its own if there is insufficient time for the complete tour. The main fea-

ture is the well preserved Neptune's Staircase, the six locks of the second Canal which lifted ships up and down the escarpment. It is sad to note the state of neglect of one of the mightiest and oldest engineering achievements in this country. The neglect does not detract, however, from the feeling of awe in observing the insides of the two lower locks. Large blocks of dolomitic limestone were quarried locally and shaped and pegged together by Scottish stonemasons. These locks, which still stand today and are resisting erosion and weathering better than the concrete locks of the fourth Canal, are a testament to these artisans of the past. The tow path was located on the south side of the Canal and the raceway and industries were on the north side.

Two delightful ivy-covered lockkeepers cottages dating from the early 1850s survive today. The cottage at 135 Bradley Street, which is designated provincially as a historical structure, is constructed of fieldstones of red Grimsby sandstone, which contrast to the grey dolostone of the locks. The other cottage is at 77-79 Bradley Street.

12. Thorold. Proceed south along Bradley, crossing over Townline Road, turning left onto St. David's Road, and immediately right onto Front Street. On the northwest corner of St. David's Road and Bradley Street, note the grand three-storey mansion named Maplehurst, built in 1856 by John Keefer, the son of the first President of the Welland Canal. Turn right at Clairmont Street. To the south lies Beaverdams Battlefield Park, a linear park constructed over the second Canal. Lock 25 has been partially uncovered and has been incorporated into the rather unique setting of a bandstand amphitheatre. The park contains several plaques and other Canal, as well as War of 1812, memorabilia.

The northeast side of the first and second Canals was heavily industrialized from Welland Vale to Thorold. In the Town of Thorold, many industrial products were manufactured, with pulp and paper eventually gaining dominance. When the third Canal was routed east of the city in the 1870s, the second Canal remained open to ship traffic from the south until about 1915, at which time it was infilled.

Turn right on Towpath Street and right again on Albert Street. An old Fire hall complete with tower, built in the late 1870s, is located almost immediately on the left at number 12. The route now passes into east Thorold with its many attractive, old residential buildings. Drive to the very end of Albert and park and walk east past the end of the street to a park bench that offers a panoramic overview of the Welland Canal and the flight locks. This is a favourite spot of ours from which to watch ships.

13. Flight Locks. Head south along Chapel Street for two blocks and turn left and left again to head north along Government Road next to the modern Canal. Note Lock 7 on your right. Within a few hundred metres are the adjoining flight locks, numbers 4, 5, and 6. This is well worth a stop and, because the locks are twinned, you can often see ships simultaneously climbing and descending the escarpment. Continuing north along Government Road and crossing Glendale Avenue soon brings you back to Lock 3, where you started this voyage into the history of the Welland Canals.

More Information

There are numerous sources of information on the Welland Canal. A particularly interesting book is *The Four Welland Canals – A Journey of Discovery in St. Catharines and Thorold* by John N. Jackson, a historian and retired professor from Brock University, who is the pre-eminent authority on the history of the Canal. The book traces the route of Tour 5 and provides a detailed look at the history and current operation of the Welland Canal.

Chapter 8

THE ERIE CANAL: YESTERDAY'S HIGHWAY

Old locks at Lockport

Background

Looking at a modern map covered with a tangle of interstate highways and railways, it is hard to imagine that in the late 1700s the USA was a land divided into east and west. The Appalachian Mountains formed a formidable barrier to travel and effectively isolated the fertile interior and the Great Lakes from the thriving eastern seaboard.

Gouverneur Morris, a member of the First Continental Congress, was one of the earliest to recognize the importance of creating an easy passage through this mountain barrier. His vision was to construct a canal along the Mohawk River valley in upper New York State. The canal, by linking New York City via the Hudson River to Lake Erie on the Great Lakes, would allow the interior to become settled and would open up trade between the east and west, thus releasing the enormous potential of this bountiful nation.

Famous Last Words

Not everyone was in favour of building the Erie Canal. Here are the words of President Thomas Jefferson in 1809. "You talk of making a canal 350 miles long through wilderness? It is little short of madness to think of it. The idea is 100 years ahead of its time. You might as well try to build a ladder to the moon."

In 1792, the Western Inland Lock Navigation Company was formed to build a canal from the Hudson River to

Lake Ontario. Money and enthusiasm, unfortunately, were soon eaten up by the rocky and rough Mohawk River. But small locks and a canal were constructed around one of the falls and a short section of the passage that eased the way for settlers to head west along this popular route. Although crude and only partly completed, the work gave a tantalizing glimpse of what a real waterway along this route could achieve.

However, the prospect of paying for the construction of a 363 mile (585 kilometre) canal through very difficult wilderness did not sit well with the tax-paying public. Fortunately, the mayor of New York City, DeWitt Clinton, stepped forth to champion the cause of the Canal and from that time until his death, no one worked harder or contributed more to the success of this project. In 1817, Clinton was elected governor of New York State, and later that year, the state legislature approved the building of the Erie Canal.

On July 4, 1817, in the village of Rome in the wilderness near the upper reaches of the Mohawk River, the construction of the Erie Canal was started. It was a formidable challenge as no canal of this length had ever been built before, certainly not through the difficult wilderness that was encountered here.

From Lake Erie to the Hudson River, the canal was to be 363 miles (585 kilometres) long. The channel was to be 40 feet (12 metres) wide at the surface and would slope inward to 28 feet (8.5 metres) at the bottom; the water would be four feet (1.2

metres) deep. Eighty-three locks were required to allow for the elevation drop of 568 feet (173 metres) between Lake Erie and the Hudson River (actually, boats would need to travel a vertical distance of 688 feet (210 metres), considering the ups and downs included in crossing valleys). A ten-foot (3-metre) wide towpath was needed along the entire length of the canal for the horses and mules to pull the canalboats. As the canal could not run through existing, flowing streams, it paralleled the Mohawk River in many places, requiring the construction of walls and dikes.

In October 1819, over two years after the first groundbreaking ceremony, the first stretch of canal – a mere 15 miles (24 kilometres) in length – was officially opened. Although critics scoffed, much more than the 15 miles had been achieved and progress continued well. One of the main obstacles was at Lockport, where the canal had to descend more than 60 feet (18 metres) down the cliff-like Niagara Escarpment. The solution was a double set of five locks to allow travel in both directions. Cut out of solid rock, these were the only set of double locks on the canal.

The Lockport locks were completed in June 1825, and soon afterward, water was let into the western 140 miles (225 kilometres) of canal. Only a few unfinished jobs remained including the construction of three weigh locks so that boats could be weighed to determine the amount of toll they must pay.

In spite of considerable technical obstacles and political opposition, the canal was completed on schedule and was opened with a fanfare so great that it is hard to imagine today. On October 26, 1825 Governor Clinton and other dignitaries boarded the Seneca Chief in Buffalo and entered the canal. At that moment a cannon was fired, then another one a few miles down the canal was fired. This cannonade progressed down the canal until it reached New York City, where a tremendous artillery salute was triggered. Then the line of gunners sent the salutes back along the same path to Buffalo to acknowledge receipt of the great news.

On arriving in New York City a week later, Governor Clinton was met by city officials and an armada of boats with tooting whistles. That day New York City had one of the greatest celebrations in its history. One part of the festivities involved pouring two kegs of Lake Erie water, which had been brought aboard the Seneca Chief, into the ocean, along with waters from mighty rivers such as the Mississippi, Thames, La Plata, Indus, Columbia, Seine, Rhine, Amazon, Nile, and Ganges in a "wedding of the waters" ceremony.

From the moment the Erie Canal opened, its waters were thick with boats carrying people and cargo. The country had never seen anything like it. There was a constant bustle of emigrants and manufactured goods moving to the west and the produce of farms and forests moving eastward. A canal craze took over the country, and not only did people clamour to ride on the Erie Canal, but many other canal projects were started in northeastern USA. Fifteen years after the Erie was opened, there were more than 4,000 miles of canals in the nation. Although many canals were built, none could compare to the success of the Erie Canal – there was only one Big Ditch.

Nathan S. Roberts, Builder of the Locks
Nathan Roberts was the man who had the unenviable task of bringing the Erie Canal up the rock face at Lockport. He was a self-made engineer and had no previous experience in canal building. With no one to assist him and no guidance except for a few books, he designed a double set of five locks. He considered the acceptance of his design as the most triumphant moment of his career.

After completion of the canal, some visionaries recognized the potential for its waters to generate power for industrial development. This was particularly the case in Lockport, where the canal descended the steep Niagara Escarpment. Lyman Spalding, a merchant, developer, and builder, did much to harness and develop the hydraulic power of the canal, which led to numerous mills and other industries being established in Lockport. Many relics of this cheap power, such as mills and raceways can be seen today and are included in the walking tour of Lockport (see below). Another Lockport visionary was Birdsill Holly, an inventor, who was a friend of Thomas Edison and helped him set up an electrical system that conducted power generated from the Lockport Raceway to industries on both sides of the canal.

Commerce thrived on the Erie Canal. In 1845, approximately 4,000 boats travelled the canal with about 25,000 people working on them. In addition, there was a large force of locktenders, towpath walkers, and repair and maintenance crews, not to mention the numerous shops and services that lined the canal. Towns sprang up where only wilderness previously existed, and cities like New York, Syracuse, and Buffalo blossomed. The country was in the grip of canal mania.

With its immense popularity, it was not long before improvements were demanded. Starting in 1836, extra sets of locks were added, all locks were extended from 90 to 180 feet (27 to 55 metres), the channel was widened and deepened to seven feet (2.1 metres), and many parts of the canal were straightened and relocated. After this enlargement was completed in 1862, the canal could carry boats of up to 250 tons.

Bygone Canal Terms

In the heyday of the Erie Canal, everyone knew what these words meant. How many of them do you recognize?

Canawler:	a name for those who worked on the canal.
Cuddy:	sleeping bunk on a canal boat.
Flying Weight:	a name for boats travelling empty.
Hoggee:	a driver of a mule team pulling a boat; often a young boy.
Hoodledasher:	an empty canal boat tied to a loaded boat.
Packet:	a passenger boat drawn by horses.
Snubbing post:	a post along the canal used to tie up boats.

But the glory days of the canals were, like the beauty of a butterfly, a brief ephemeral thing. By 1850, the nemesis of the canals, the steam locomotive, had arrived. No new canals were under construction, and many of the existing ones fell into neglect.

Although the canal era was well past by this time, the Erie Canal kept on going strong. Passenger traffic on the canal could not compete with railways, however, the Erie performed well carrying heavy cargo, where speed was not an important factor.

In 1882, all tolls were abolished as the Erie had paid its original cost many times over. Beginning in 1903, the Erie Canal and its two main branches, the Champlain and Oswego Canals, were deepened and widened and larger locks were installed. At Lockport, the eastbound set of locks were abandoned and are now a series of five waterfalls. The "flight of five" westbound locks were replaced by Locks 34 and 35. These locks are the only double locks of the 57 on the new canal and provide a combined lift of 49 feet (15 metres). Much of the old Erie Canal was relocated, and the new system, completed in 1918, was renamed the New York State Barge Canal.

Where horse-drawn packet boats once sailed, huge barges, almost 300 feet (91 metres) long, are now nudged along by diesel tug boats. The romance of the by-gone era is now only a memory, and the role of Clinton's Ditch is quietly evolving to one of a recreational waterway.

TOUR 1:
A Leisurely Drive Along the Old Erie Canal (Map 10)

For a wonderfully serene and peaceful afternoon that brings peace to the soul and offers a nostalgic look back at yesteryear, this tour can't be beat. There is something soothing about a ribbon of water that meanders through the countryside and at every turn offers delightful scenes such as a pleasure craft slowly puttering along with a long delicate wake trailing behind, the reflection of a stately tree gently undulating in the water, a couple walking hand-in-hand along the towpath, or a small boy and his father casting fishing lines into the water. Rush and haste, although the daily norm in its hey day, are now totally out of place along this quiet backwater. Instead of industry, green space and parks now line the canal, where hours can be spent on picnics, watching the ripple of the water, and relaxing in a quiet way that is so hard to find these days.

This tour is about 50 miles (80 kilometres) long and will take at least half a day. Starting from Niagara Falls, New York, proceed south along the Robert Moses Parkway and then River Road (Highway 384) into North Tonawanda, which marks the western entrance to the Erie Canal, now called the New York State Barge Canal. Be sure to not cross the canal, also known as Tonawanda Creek at this point, as the tour follows the north shore of the canal along Sweeny Street. The tour is shown in Map 10.

This part of North Tonawanda is unappealing and run-down with that

Traveller's Tip – Sustenance
One of the more pleasant aspects of a day trip is the pause for a bite to eat when, over a chilled glass of Chardonnay or a mug of ale, one can ponder the miles that lie behind and plan the miles ahead. Unfortunately, this tour is depressingly devoid of establishments that offer the charm or atmosphere for such interludes. Instead, we recommend you pack a picnic lunch and enjoy one of the many delightful parks along the canal.

tired, hang-dog look of a place that has seen better days. In 1823, a dam was built across Tonawanda Creek to raise the water level for the Erie Canal, which opened two years later. In the 1800's, Tonawanda became the lumber capital of the world and

Lift bridge with concrete-block counter-weight

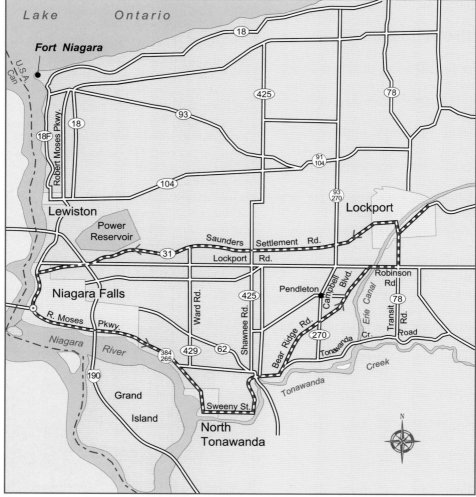

Map 10, A Leisurely Drive Along the Old Erie Canal

the shoreline of Whites Island was thick with stacks of white pine planks awaiting shipment to shipyards on the east coast.

Proceeding eastward along Sweeny Street, you will shortly come across the dark hulk of the lift bridge for the New York Central Railway with its gigantic concrete-block counter-weight looming against the skyline. The bridge was built around 1919 and still sees service today. On the north side of Sweeny Street are some old brick industrial buildings. Inset on the wall of one, an inscription gives a reminder of the past glory of this city: "Power House, Buffalo & Niagara Falls Electric Railway, 1895."

To the east of North Tonawanda, the canal is dotted with lovely parks and marinas. One of the best places to stop and inspect the canal more closely is the Botanical Gardens of North Tonawanda, which are on the right-hand side of the road on the outskirts of the city.

Follow along beside the canal until you reach Bear Ridge Road, which angles off to the left and takes you into the town of Pendleton. Note the change in architectural style as there are quite a number of large modern middle-class homes along this stretch of the road.

An 1840 cobblestone home is located on the left-hand side at 6952 Bear Ridge Road before the lights at Campbell Boulevard. This quaint Cape Cod cottage, with its finish of small water-washed stones on the front and larger stones on the side, was the home of Gideon Browning. Note the interesting side lights at the front door.

If you would like more information on the Pendleton area, turn left on Campbell Boulevard and proceed to the log cabin at number 6570, which is home to the Pendleton Historical Society. The building houses a number of historical artifacts, and talking to the members can give a fascinating insight into yesteryear. But plan your visit carefully as the centre is only open on Sundays between 2 and 4 pm. Return to Bear Ridge Road and proceed into Lockport.

There are two particularly noteworthy areas in Lockport. The first, a district of stately trees and magnificent mansions, is a well kept secret that is rarely discovered by tourists. Grand Victorian estates such as these are rarely found even in much larger urban centres and are monuments to the enormous wealth that the canal brought to this city.

On entering Lockport from the

Power house inscription

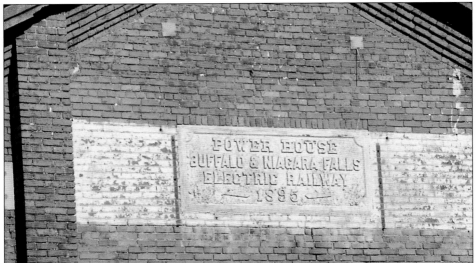

south along Highway 78, turn right on Lincoln Avenue. Turn left on Pine Street and circle the block on your right contained by Pine Street, Willow Street, Locust Street, and Lincoln Avenue. Along Willow Street you will note some remnants of streets and sidewalks made of bricks. These homes were built mostly in the 1870s by people who made their wealth directly and indirectly from the Erie Canal: owners of mills and factories, generators of water power, land developers, and politicians.

To inspect the interior of one of these homes, visit the Kenan Centre at 433 Locust Avenue. This gracious Victorian mansion and adjacent carriage houses have been remarkably transformed into the cultural hub of Lockport. Construction of the house began in 1850 but four years later a fire destroyed all but two walls. By 1859, the house had been totally rebuilt on the original foundation. The two-storey brick house is topped by an observatory, which offers a panoramic view of the landscaped

Mansion on Locust Street, Lockport

grounds. Four porches provide summer shade. The Centre, which accommodates classrooms, studios, art galleries, and an intimate theatre, is open from 2 to 5 pm daily. There is a year round program of art displays, concerts, plays, and other events.

Return to South Transit Street (Highway 78) and head north until you reach the canal. The second highlight of Lockport, and the reason for its fame, is the set of locks located here in the centre of the city. If you have time, you should now embark on Tour 2. If time is short, even a brief stroll along the locks is recommended.

A walk along the canal past the locks is a journey into the past. The original five locks are now spill ways and have been replaced by two larger more modern locks, which are used by pleasure craft. Descend alongside the old locks and admire the graceful grey arches and fine limestone masonry that have not lost their charm, or strength, over the 150 years since they were crafted. A small but delightful museum is located at the bottom of the locks and has many artifacts, old photographs, and brochures describing the history of the canal. Walking further along the towpath, you will pass under the so-called "upside-down" bridge and see the crumbling stone ruins of industrial plants and mills that lined the canal and used the power generated by water falling over the mountain ridge.

The central part of Lockport surrounding the locks has the rather dreary look of a place that has been left behind by modern developments.

To finish this tour, drive east on Market Street along the south shore of the canal. The first few miles are a series of lovely parks along the canal including a tree park and an exercise circuit.

> ### Traveller's Tip – Bargain-Priced Gasoline
> *Plan your trip so the gas gauge is approaching empty as you return to Niagara Falls. At the Tuscarora Indian Reservation on Highway 31, gasoline is sold at prices that are substantially lower than anywhere else in the region.*

The tour finishes on the eastern outskirts of Lockport. To return to the Niagara area you can either retrace your steps along this tour or, if you wish to return at a faster pace, return to the centre of Lockport and take Highway 31, which brings you directly into Niagara Falls.

TOUR 2:
Walking Historic Lockport (Map 11)

As you drive into Lockport along Transit Street, turn left at Park Street and find a parking spot anywhere near the intersection with Hawley Street. Follow the tour as shown in Map 11 stopping at the following historical sites. You should allow between one and two hours for this 2.2 mile (3.5 kilometre) tour.

1. Niagara County Court House. Built in 1886 of sandstone, this building was extensively renovated in 1913-1914 with the addition of the domed rotunda and Ionic portico. In 1955-58, the unattractive, but functional, west wing was added.

2. Niagara County Historical Society has its headquarters in a five-building historical complex at 215

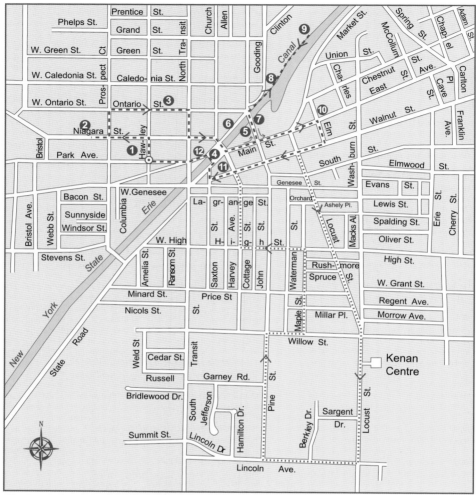

Map 11, Walking Historic Lockport

Niagara Street. The main house, named the Dr. Samuel Outwater Building in honour of the man who donated it to the Historical Society, was built in 1864 by Windsor Trowbridge who owned a brickyard where Trowbridge Street is today. The stable in the rear was remodelled into the present pioneer building. The two-room brick building called the Wash-

ington Hunt Law Office was built in 1835 and moved here from its original location on Market Street. The museum is open Thursday through Sunday, 1-5 pm and has a gift shop.

3. Colonel William Bond House at 143 Ontario Street. Built in 1823-24 by Colonel William Bond, this was the first brick house in Lockport. The house was later occupied by Mr. Jesse

Hawley, the man who persuaded Governor DeWitt Clinton that the Erie Canal should be built. Listed in the National Register of Historic Sites, it is open to the public from 1-5 pm on Thursdays, Saturdays, and Sundays from April through December and features Empire furnishings.

4. Big Bridge. At 249 feet (76 metres) across the canal by 399 feet (122 metres)parallel to the canal, this is one of the widest bridges in the world. From above, it is an unassuming and boring expanse of concrete. Down below, you can listen to your voice echo and reverberate.

5. Locks 34 and 35. Completed in 1918, the locks are still operating today, providing a lift of 50 feet (15 metres). A pleasant pastime is to watch cabin cruisers and other pleasure boats of the wealthy passing through the locks.

6. Five Flight Locks. Hewn out of solid rock, the original set of locks was completed in 1825. The twinning of the locks was finished in 1847; an expansion in size followed in 1862 with a final expansion in 1918, which saw the current configuration achieved. The old locks are now a series of five waterfalls that are best appreciated from the lower level.

7. Canal Museum. Nestled at the base of the locks, the museum offers free viewing of canal artifacts and numerous photographs of those by-gone days. Brochures describing the historic Erie Canal and Lockport are also available.

8. Ruins of Holly Manufacturing Company. Continuing a little past the locks along the towpath, you will see the crumbling stone ruins along the sides of the steep slope. These are all that remain of the factory owned by Birdsill Holly, a friend of Thomas Edison who helped him set up an electrical system to deliver power from the Lockport Raceway to industries along the canal.

9. Upson Park & Industrial Ruins. Further along the towpath is Upson Park which features crumbling stone ruins of the former Lockport Pulp Mill and Hiram Benedict's boat building yard.

Retrace your steps back along the canal and head east along Main Street until you reach Elm Street. The next stop is on the northeast corner.

10. Old Post Office. Listed in the National Register of Historic Places, this outstanding example of early 20th century public architecture was built in 1902-1904 from a design by James Knox Taylor. Now under private ownership, the building was restored in 1992.

Optional: If you did not visit the mansions district as part of the driving tour and if time allows and you are a hardy walker, head south on Locust Street and circle the block contained by Pine Street, Willow Street, Locust Street, and Lincoln Avenue. A visit to the Kenan Centre at 433 Locust Avenue, which is housed in a gracious Victorian mansion and adjacent carriage houses is recommended (see Tour 1 for details). A word of caution: This is a long side trip, (about 1.9 miles; 3.0 kilometres) so you may prefer to do it by car (or bicycle).

11. YMCA Building at 32 cottage Street. Built in 1835 by Gillette

Bacon, this building served as a refuge for slaves from the south during the Civil War and as Lockport's headquarters for the Red Cross during World War I. The property was acquired by the YMCA in 1927.

12. Upson Coal Company Building at 8 and 10 West Main Street, constructed of field stones, is a unique wedge shape to fit its narrow lot next to the canal. Built in 1902, it was moved 32 feet (10 metres) to the west in 1910 to make room for the Big Bridge. Henry Schmidt, the great grandson of the original Upson, now uses the building for his law practice.

More Information

An illustrated brochure, "Lockport New York, Historic Jewel of the Erie Canal", describing Lockport and the history of the Erie Canal and including a map of Lockport, is available by calling Niagara County Tourism at 1-800-338-7890.

Ruins of Holly Manufacturing Company

Chapter 9

THE BRUCE TRAIL: HIKING THE BACKBONE OF NIAGARA

The Bruce Trail has probably inflicted more blisters, sore feet, and aching backs than any other trail in North America. But the aches and pains are well worth it as hiking the Bruce Trail, stretching 773 kilometres (480 miles) from Queenston Heights in the south to Tobermory at the northern end of the Bruce Peninsula, is a beautiful and rewarding experience.

The trail follows the cliffs of the Niagara Escarpment, a ribbon of near wilderness running through one of the most populated parts of the country. More than just a long ridge of rock, the escarpment is a vital natural link, which ties together a rich tapestry of plant assemblages, bird life, animals, picturesque villages, and history. In recognition of its international importance as an ecosystem and its exceptional scenic beauty, the Niagara Escarpment was named a World Biosphere Reserve in 1990 by the United Nations Educational, Scientific, and Cultural Organization. It joined a select group of Biosphere Reserves, including the Galapagos Islands, the Serengeti National Park, and the Florida Everglades.

The idea of the Bruce Trail began in 1960. Today, it has become an important component of the provincial Niagara Escarpment Plan and

Bruce Trail Cairn at Queenston Heights

links parks and natural features. In the Niagara area, with its high urban and agricultural development, the Bruce Trail offers an escape into the natural world. The trail is rugged in places and is punctuated by waterfalls cascading over steep dolostone cliffs. The Bruce Trail is more than a place to hike. It is also a link between delightful parks and conservation areas, some of which are described below, that often contain nature trails and points of interest; they also form excellent bases for hiking the Bruce.

A detailed guide book to the Trail is available from the Bruce Trail Association (see Appendix). Here we do not describe the Bruce Trail in its entirety through the Niagara area but, instead, describe selected portions that give good overviews of the natural setting of this region.

Although frowned upon by the Bruce Trail Association, a number of people do enjoy the Trail using mountain bikes. If you plan to bike the Trail, remember that hikers have priority and be careful – there are some steep and rocky sections.

The Trail is marked with white blazes; that is, white rectangles that are approximately 6 inches (15 centimetres) high and 2 inches (5 centimetres) wide have been painted on trees, fence posts, and rocks. A turn is indicated by a pair of blazes, one above the other, with the upper one offset in the direction of the turn. In the Niagara area, there are numerous side trails that lead to various points of interest. These are also marked, but with blue or yellow blazes. For various reasons, the Bruce Trail does get re-routed occasionally, especially in highly populated areas such as the Niagara region. In case of doubt, always follow the white blazes.

We must offer a word of caution – it is very easy to get lost on the Bruce Trail. In the Niagara area, the vegetation grows lush and thick, often obscuring blazes and trail junctions. Due to the high population density, there are many other trails, some of which are more dominant than the Bruce. Always keep in contact with the white blazes. If you have not seen a blaze for a hundred or two hundred metres, you should backtrack until you find the correct path.

TOUR 1
Brock's Monument to Woodend Conservation Area (Map 12)

This beautiful 18 kilometre (11 mile) outing is one of our favorite hikes and offers an excellent introduction to the Niagara Escarpment. As a linear route it can be done in either direction, although we will describe it from east to west. There are good picnic facilities and ample parking areas at either end.

The start (or finish, if you prefer to do this tour in reverse) is at the Bruce Trail cairn at the east end of Queenston Park (see Chapter 5). Map 12 shows the route and a brief summary is provided below. Note that distances from the starting point are given in square brackets, for example, [5.5 km; 3.4 miles]:

➤ Cross Queenston Heights Park going west along the brow of the escarpment.

This first section contains a tour within a tour: the Queenston Trails, which is marked by signposts and provides a wonderful insight into the historical Queenston Quarry. Queenston Trails can be done either on its own or as part of Tour 1 to Woodend. If you only have time for a short excursion, but you want to capture a flavour of the Niagara Escarpment and some of the history of this area, then Queenston Trails is highly recommended.

The first Queenston Trails signpost occurs at about kilometre 2 (mile 1.2). If you are only interested in walking Queenston Trails, an alternative (shorter) start is by driving west from Brock's Monument along Portage Road about 1.7 km (1.1 miles) to the second small parking lot. Walk north along the trail and turn left (west) when you reach the Bruce Trail. You will encounter the first signpost in about 0.5 km (0.3 miles). The following signposts are shown on Map 12. Vandals occasionally remove some of these posts, but don't despair if some are missing; with sharp eyes you will be able to spot the features.

1. View of St. Davids. From here you will have a magnificent panorama of the plain below the escarpment with its orchards, vineyards, and tilled fields that stretch to Lake Ontario on the horizon.

2. The Abandoned Tower. This landmark was erected by the Department of National Defence in 1951/52, probably to intercept American radio waves.

3. Foundations of Worker's Village. Fourteen houses were built here in 1897 to house workers for the Queenston Quarries.

4. & 8. These areas show evidence of quarrying activity that preceded the opening of Queenston Quarry in about 1840. Scottish masons retrieved top quality stones

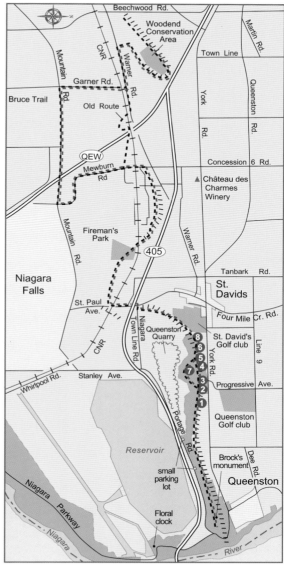

Map 12, Brock's Monument to Woodend Conservation Area (note that north is to the right)

from these locations; the blocks you see are rejects. Quarrying in those early days was done on the edge of the escarpment so the rocks could be easily rolled over the edge.

5. This old moss-covered limestone block on the south side of the trail shows evidence of the quarrying method using steel wedges, called plugs and feathers, that were pounded into holes bored into the stone. Large rectangular blocks were split off and shipped throughout eastern Canada.

6. In 1882, Isaac Usher & Son opened a cement operation at this site. The Ushers mined into a natural layer of rock cement, fired it in limestone kilns, ground it into a powder, and barrelled the final product. Facing stiff competition from Portland cement, the Usher operation closed in 1905.

7. Limestone Caverns. A detour from the main path to visit these caves is well worth the effort. Not only do you get a look at these "caves," which actually have formed largely by quarrying, but you also get a close-up look at the mammoth pit left by Queenston Quarry. A unique feature of the cavern is the flat roof, the petrified mud floor of an ancient shallow sea.

An informative brochure describing the Queenston Trails interpretive walk is available from the Niagara Parks Commission (see Appendix).

➢ About 3 km (1.8 miles) from the starting cairn, the Bruce Trail descends to the bottom of the escarpment.

➢ Follow the railway bed of the former New York Central Railway, emerging at the intersection of Townline Road and Creek Road [5.5 km; 3.4 miles from cairn at start].

➢ Go south along Four Mile Creek Road passing under Highway 405. Halfway up the hill turn right into the woods. The trail then enters Fireman's Park [7.4 km; 4.6 miles], which has toilets and parking.

➢ The trail climbs back up the escarpment; when you reach Mewburn Road, head south until you reach Mountain Road. Turn right, crossing the QEW Highway, and proceed to Garner Road [14.9 km; 9.2 miles]. Turn right and walk to Warner Road, turn left and go for about 1.0 km (0.6 miles).

As an aside, it should be mentioned that previously the Bruce Trail crossed the QEW Highway via a railway bridge (the old path is shown on Map 12). Due to incomprehensible bureaucratic logic, the railway no longer allows right of way across its bridge, causing this very long and boring detour.

➢ Turn right into the woods and proceed past a vineyard to a road that leads into Woodend Conservation area.

➢ Turn right following the trail in a loop around the Woodend Conservation Area (described separately below).

If you have energy and curiosity left, you may choose to follow the Bruce Trail further west. A convenient place to stop is at the intersection of the old Welland Canal and Glendale Avenue, about 0.5 km (0.3 miles) to the east of the new Canal, for a hiking distance of about 23 km (14 miles). If you wish to proceed even further, then a convenient stopping spot is Brock University, yielding a distance of 30 km (19 miles).

TOUR 2

Woodend Conservation Area

Woodend, the terminus of Tour 1, occupies 45 hectares (112 acres) on top of a narrow promontory or nose of the Niagara Escarpment and is well worth a visit on its own rights. St. Anthony's Nose, as it was originally called, was settled in 1779 by the United Empire Loyalist family of Peter Lampman. Their home had a magnificent view of the plain below and Lake Ontario. A gun battery commanded the viewpoint during the War of 1812. Archibald Lampman, the grandson of the initial settler, was a frequent visitor and wrote several poems about the area. Sections of

Decew Falls

the original two houses were incorporated into the present building, which was finished in 1932.

The area is a lovely example of Carolinian forest, consisting largely of broad-leaf hardwood species such as sugar maple, beech, red oak, white oak, and bur oak. Other species include black walnut, sycamore, white oak, shagbark hickory, and rock elm. The occasional tulip tree, black cherry, black oak, and paw paw are also found here. Chipmunks, grey and red squirrels, skunks, mice, and raccoons are common at Woodend. Frequently sighted birds include the blue-jay, mourning dove, robin, woodpecker, and many species of swallow and sparrow. In addition,

Morningstar Mill

Woodend offers good exposures of the rock strata that form the Escarpment.

Woodend, with its sweeping views of orchards and vineyards, is an excellent spot for a picnic. It also offers hiking, cross-country skiing, and bird watching and generally is a delightful place to commune with nature.

A leaflet, which includes a map, is available from the Niagara Peninsula Conservation Authority.

TOUR 3
DeCew Falls and Morningstar Mill

This is one of our favorite spots with its picturesque waterfall and historic mill. The site is located on Decew Road, a little west of the intersection with Merrittville (No. 50) Highway in the southern outskirts of St. Catharines. This site is on the Bruce Trail and is a good starting point for hikes. It is also a good staging area for bicycle tours southward into the Short Hills, St. Johns, and Effingham. We often see white-tailed deer in this area.

The mill was built of local stone in 1872 on the site of a former blacksmith and carpentry shop. Water was diverted from Beaverdams Creek to power the mill. Several millers leased the mill, and in 1883, it was purchased by Wilson Morningstar, after whom it is named. Destroyed by fire in 1895, it was rebuilt and operated continuously until 1933. It then fell into disrepair but has recently been reconstructed and made into a museum.

A highlight of this stop is DeCew Falls, which cascade 22 metres (72 feet) into a bowl-shaped amphitheatre just behind the mill. In days gone by, this was a popular spot to visit. There was a large spiral staircase leading into the gorge from 1890 to 1910. Today, the area is generally unfrequented, and you can enjoy it in peace and quiet. Proceed a few hundred metres along the Bruce Trail toward the east and look for a place to scramble down into the gorge. Although steep, you will be rewarded by a wonderful view of the falls. For a special treat, you can go behind the falls and feel the cool spray.

The Bruce Trail continues eastward, passes a large reservoir which supplies water for the DeCew Hydroelectric power station, one of the oldest in Canada, and then wends its way to Brock University. You can follow the Bruce Trail or go east along Decew Road to the stone remains of a house built by Captain John Decew. This house served as the headquarters for the British in this area during the War of 1812, and it was to this house that Laura Secord made her famous walk from Queenston.

Hiking westward from Morningstar Mill, you will gradually descend the Niagara Escarpment and enter into Short Hills Provincial Park. This is an interesting area where the normally linear escarpment has been broken into a jumble of hills and valleys. Deer are a relatively common sight as you hike up and down along this stretch of the Bruce Trail.

16 Mile Creek tumbles over the escarpment

TOUR 4
Louth Conservation Area

As the Bruce Trail wends its way westward from DeCew Falls, there are several delightful conservation areas. The first is at Rockway, about five kilometres (3 miles) southwest of St. Catharines on Pelham Road (Regional Road 89), where there is a pleasant side loop of the Bruce Trail. Park at the Rockway Community Centre and look for the Bruce Trail on the east side of the building.

But the hiking is even better if you drive about two kilometres (1 mile) further west along Pelham Road. When the road forks, bear right (onto Regional Road 669) and take the first right turn onto Staff Road. Proceed a few hundred meters to the sign-posted Louth Conservation Area and its small parking lot.

Follow the blue blazes (signifying a side branch of the Bruce) to the edge of the escarpment, where you join the main Bruce Trail. This is a wonderful area at any time of year, with its green moss-covered boulders and crevassed, ominous landscape. But in the spring the forest floor is covered with a sea of delicate white trilliums as well as Dutchman's britches and trout lilies. We suggest you make a loop excursion by bearing right onto the side trail (blue blazes) at this point and doing the loop in a counter

Old log cabin at Ball's Falls

clock-wise direction. The trail takes you first eastward along the top edge of the escarpment, then down a path along an old roadbed, then through Carolinian forest. The highlight of the outing is a waterfall where the waters of Sixteen Mile Creek tumble over the limestone crags of the escarpment. This hidden beauty spot is seldom visited, even by locals, and is a suitable reward for venturing off the beaten track.

TOUR 5
Ball's Falls Historical Park and Conservation Area *(Map 13)*

Ball's Falls is a pearl suspended on the string of the Bruce Trail. Once an early 19th century industrial hamlet, this site, perched on the edge of the escarpment, features an operational mill, two waterfalls, numerous historic buildings, and lovely nature trails. Map 13 shows the Balls Falls area.

To reach Ball's Falls, exit the Queen Elizabeth Highway at Vineland. Follow Victoria Avenue (Highway 24) south to Regional Road 24, where you turn eastward and travel to Ball's Falls.

Restored and maintained by the Niagara Peninsula Conservation Authority, the site occupies over 80 hectares (200 acres) of the original 480 hectares (1200 acres) purchased by the Ball brothers in 1807. George Ball constructed grist, saw, and wool mills, which lead to the growth of one of the first communities in this area. The hamlet was known as Ball's Mills, Louth Mills, Glen Elgin, and finally as Ball's Falls because of the two delightful cataracts on the property. In the

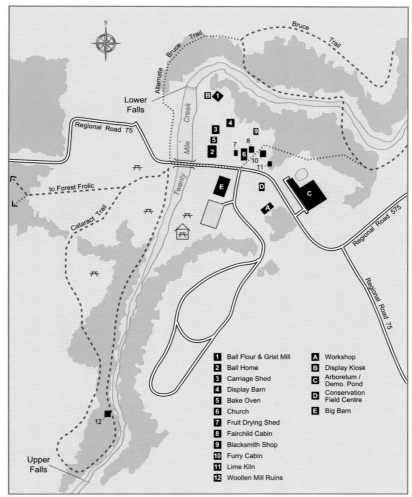

Legend:

1 Ball Flour & Grist Mill
2 Ball Home
3 Carriage Shed
4 Display Barn
5 Bake Oven
6 Church
7 Fruit Drying Shed
8 Fairchild Cabin
9 Blacksmith Shop
10 Furry Cabin
11 Lime Kiln
12 Woollen Mill Ruins

A Workshop
B Display Kiosk
C Arboretum / Demo. Pond
D Conservation Field Centre
E Big Barn

Map 13, Ball's Falls Historical Park and Conservation Area

mid 1800s, however, significant developments such as the railway and the Welland Canal led to the rapid growth of other villages below the escarpment, and by the turn of the century, most of the activity at Ball's Falls had ceased.

Ball's Falls has been lovingly restored to its early 1800s atmosphere and now features an operating flour mill, a lime kiln, a church, family home, blacksmith shop, carriage shed, and more. In addition to its historical interest, Ball's Falls is also a centre for nature activities, offering a tremendous diversity of flora and fauna as well as excellent exposures of geologic strata.

The Bruce Trail passes through the very north end of the conservation area to the north of the lower falls. Hikes along the Bruce Trail either to the west or the east can be made from this location.

Our favorite trail at Ball's Falls is the Cataract Trail, which starts from the west side of the bridge across Twenty Mile Creek and meanders in a loop to the Upper Falls and back. One leg is along the Creek and the other is inland, offering a wide range of plant species and scenery. The falls tumble delightfully over a high cliff and can be viewed at close proximity from above or below. The character of the falls changes dramatically with the seasons, ranging from a raging torrent in the spring to a thin veil in late summer.

Other trails provide access to view the Lower Falls and to explore the rest of the conservation area.

TOUR 6
Cave Springs

No book on Niagara would be complete without a mention of Cave Springs, the setting for the most enchanting folklore in these parts. Cave Springs is under the care and management of Margaret Reed, who sold the property to the Niagara Peninsula Conservation Authority. Ms Reed, a delightful character who guards the sanctity of Cave Springs with a fierce determination, has fostered the growth of Carolinian forest

Aerial view of Upper Ball's Falls

NIAGARA PENINSULA CONSERVATION AUTHORITY

Boy jumping over Upper Ball's Falls

on the property and has about 60 species including the endangered cucumber tree. She gives historical tours to school groups and other interested parties with a particular focus on environmental issues. Access to Cave Springs is by appointment only (905 563-6353).

So what are some of the intriguing legends associated with Cave Springs? There are stories of a lost cave that contains untold riches in Indian artifacts. One night before the turn of the century, Emerson Grobb, a local farmer, was returning home after an evening of carousing. Apparently he fell into a cave while taking a short cut through the Cave Springs farm and spent the night there. In the morning he was amazed to find himself surrounded by Indian relics and rushed home with an earthenware pot that today resides in the Royal Ontario Museum. Excited by his find, he returned to the site but, alas, was not able to find the Lost Cave. To this day, the cave has resisted all efforts to re-discover it.

The site is also of considerable historical significance. A village belonging to the Neutral Indians is thought to have been situated here. Several artifacts that provide clues about these ancient people have been found at Cave Springs. One of the most interesting is a unique set of Indian heads carved into the rock near the top of the escarpment. Excellent examples of the artisanship of the Neutral Indians and the only such stone figures in Ontario, these carvings have been destroyed by vandals. Fortunately, a plaster cast was made of one of the heads and today resides in Lundy's Lane Museum in Niagara Falls.

Crafts at Ball's Falls

The story of Cave Springs farm begins in 1798, when the land was granted to Haramanus ("Harmonious") House, a private in the famed Butler's Rangers of the American Revolutionary War. The first house was likely built on the site where the barn is located now. Today the vineyards of Cave Spring Cellars are located in this picturesque area.

Two natural wonders have added to the fame of Cave Springs. One is a magnesium-sulphate- rich spring. Magnesium sulphate is the working ingredient of Epsom Salts and acts as both an antacid and a laxative. Thus, both Indians and early settlers alike prized the pure spring water for its therapeutic qualities. Today the spring has been diverted to the neighbouring United Church Camp.

The other natural phenomenon is an ice cave that retains its ice through most of the summer. Used as a cold storage by early settlers, it was largely destroyed by an enterprising individual who blew it up whilst trying to enlarge the entrance so it would make a more accessible tourist attraction. Visits are still made to the cave, but now they are with climbing ropes and crampons.

Many other mysteries surround Cave Springs and its niche in the escarpment. There is folklore about an underground lake, about German spies during the war, and much more. The interested reader should refer to W.F. Rannie's book *Cave Springs Farm – In Lore and Legend*, or better yet, make an appointment to see the site and hear about it directly from Margaret Reed.

Chapter 10

SHORT HILLS

The landscape in the Short Hills area is quite unlike anywhere else in Niagara. It has been moulded into a jumble of small but steep hills and valleys by the last ice age. With its varied topography, enchanting woods, winding lanes, and historic buildings, Short Hills is a delightful area for walking, bicycling, and car touring.

TOUR 1:
Exploring Short Hills (Map 14)

Myriads of charming excursions can be made here, and this one is included to pique your interest and encourage you to get out and explore what we consider the prettiest area in Niagara.

This tour, which can be enjoyed on foot or by bicycle or car, is about 10 kilometres (six miles) long and can be done at any time of year. The starting point is the St. John Outdoor Education Centre (formerly a schoolhouse) at the corner of Holland and Hollow Roads. If you are not sure how to get there, refer to the instructions for Tour 2.

The St. Johns Education Centre is surrounded by a split-rail fence, with metal plates naming the class that made each part of the fence. Should the building be open, be sure to visit the Ted Brown room, a charming replica of pioneer school life.

It is hard to believe that the tiny, sleepy hamlet of St. John was once a thriving, bustling community. The village formed around a sawmill that was built on Twelve Mile Creek in 1792. A post office was established in 1831, at which time the village boasted a woollen factory, a tannery, a foundry, stores, and several mills. Sadly, the village declined to almost nothing when the early water power of Short Hills was replaced by the greater resources and transportation convenience of the Welland Canal. The hamlet, although greatly reduced in size from its hey day, has retained its picturesque charm.

Walk west along Holland Road (the name changes to Roland Road), which winds down into a pretty valley and Twelve Mile Creek and then up into open country. Short Hills Provincial Park lies to the right of the road and is well worth a visit (see Tour 3). The sharp of eye will observe abundant bird life throughout this walk. Turn left into Sulphur Springs Drive, a narrow tree-lined road that is cool in summer, brilliant in fall, and serene in winter. A beautifully restored red brick farmhouse is on the right. Before turning left onto Orchard Hill Road, you may wish to proceed a little further along Sulphur Springs Drive and enjoy the view of a

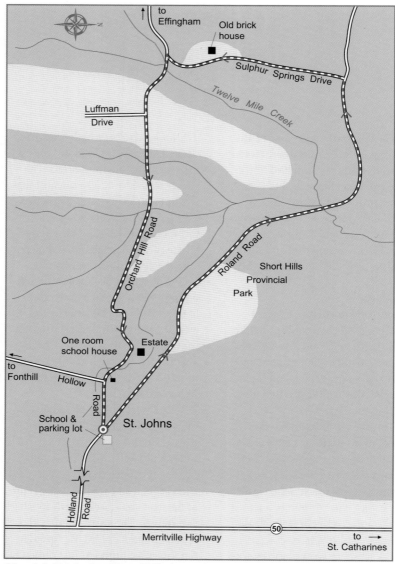

Map 14, Exploring Short Hills (note that north is to the right)

stream cascading merrily along beside the road. Return to Orchard Hill Road and stroll along this hilly route. It rolls up and down, reminding your tired legs why this area is called Short Hills, until it brings you back to Hollow Road. An historic one-room schoolhouse, which was used from 1804 to 1844, stands at the junction. Turn left and you are soon back at the starting point.

TOUR 2:
The St. Johns Conservation Area and the Sassafras Stroll *(Map 15)*

If you are looking for a quiet place, an oasis of solitude, where you can commune with nature and escape the hectic, stressful pace of our modern society, you have no further to go than the St. Johns Conservation area. This secluded forest area, nestled in the Short Hills, offers the perfect retreat for nature lovers, hikers, bird watchers, and fishermen.

Tucked into this relatively small area (31 hectares; 76 acres) are trees and shrubs of the Carolinian forests normally found in the eastern and southeastern United States rather than this far north. Because this area has never been farmed or developed, you will see rare species and trees that are over 200 years old.

Fishing at St. Johns

NIAGARA PENINSULA CONSERVATION AUTHORITY

But the jewel of this conservation area is a large pond whose still waters teem with trout. Built in 1964 to regulate the flow of water into Twelve Mile Creek, the stocked pond serves as a trout fishery and is a jealously guarded secret amongst local anglers.

This area is enchanting in all seasons, but our favorite is the spring, when the forest floor is thick with

Map 15, The St. John's Conservation Area and the Sassafras Stroll

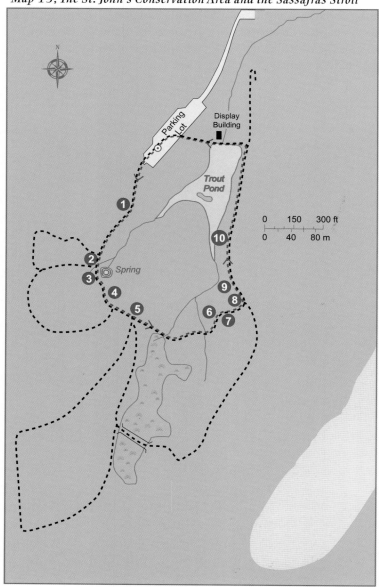

white trilliums and the sun filters through the forest canopy bathing flowers, ferns, and moss-covered logs in a soft, golden light. Trails lead deep into the forest to magical glades where elves dance and the silence is broken only by the whispering of the wind.

St. Johns, which is not easy to find, is located about 8 kilometres (5 miles) southwest of St. Catharines and about two kilometres (1.2 miles) north of Fonthill. From Fonthill, start at the intersection of Highway 20 and Pelham Street (traffic lights) and head north for about two kilometres (1.2 miles) along Pelham Street, which turns into Hollow Road. A small sign on the right-hand side of the road indicates the Conservation area. Turn left onto Barron Road and follow it about 300 m to the parking lot.

If you are coming from the north along Merrittville Highway (Highway 50), look for Holland Road, which is about 4.7 kilometres (2.9 miles) north of St. Catharines (i.e. north of St. David's Road). Follow Holland Road west 2.2 kilometres (1.4 miles) and at the Village of St. Johns turn left onto Hollow Road. Follow it south for 1.5 kilometres (0.9 miles). A small sign on the left-hand side of the road indicates the Conservation area. Turn right onto Barron Road and follow it about 300 m to the parking lot.

The Sassafras Stroll is a self-guiding nature trail that is named after the Sassafras tree that grows abundantly in this conservation area. The loop, which is over flat terrain, is shown in Map 15 and can be completed in as little as twenty minutes,

A White Trillium

The Trillium

The trillium, Ontario's official flower, is one of the most enchanting of forest flowers. In the spring, it can be found growing singly or in great masses in forests almost everywhere in North America. When it first emerges, the distinctive three-petalled flower is white. About two weeks after opening, the flower turns pink, and after about a month, it turns to a rose colour and begins to wither.

although we urge that you stroll more leisurely and enjoy the Carolinian forest.

A tornado ripped through the conservation area on May 20, 1996, causing considerable damage. (The

The Sassafras Tree

A deciduous tree found in the eastern and south-eastern US that grows to a height of 6 to 15 metres (20 to 50 feet). The leaves are elliptical or two- or three-lobed in shape, and these can all occur on the same tree. Small yellow-green flowers appear with the flowers in the spring. The leaves and bark are aromatic and the roots yield an oil that is used in soaps. Sassafras tea, a spring tonic of years gone by, is made by boiling the bark or roots.

tornado also touched down at a nearby drive-in theatre where, by coincidence, the movie "Twister" was playing.) Evidence of the enormous power of wind is seen in several places in this walk.

Niagara Ferns

The trail begins at the southwest end of the parking lot and has ten stops that are briefly summarized below and are shown on Map 15.

1. The many shrubs in this area provide food and cover for various species of birds including scarlet tanagers, rufous-sided towhees, thrushes, catbirds, and warblers.

2. This small pond fills a former gravel pit and is fed by a natural spring.

3. To the left of the trail (east side) is a forest in a young growth stage, while on the right is a mature (Maple-Beech climax) forest. The trees in the young forest are smaller and allow more light to penetrate. This stimulates growth of ground cover plants that attract birds and animals.

4. This stop features a small tangled clearing of grapevines. The vines grow up support trees which eventually die, creating the clearing.

5. Many small sassafras trees are located here. The leaves have a spicy odour when crushed, and Sassafras tea can be made from the bark or the roots.

6. The forest floor is home to fungus, moulds, mushrooms, and toadstools as well as insects such as spiders, ants, beetles. It takes about 1,000 years to make one inch of soil from the fallen leaves and branches.

7. The Rough Horsetail (or Common Scouring Rush), the most primitive member of the fern families, is found here. It does not have flowers, leaves, seeds, or true roots.

8. Several species of ferns can be seen here. Ferns are unlike any other green plants in that they do not

NIAGARA PENINSULA CONSERVATION AUTHORITY

have flowers and, therefore, can not reproduce by seeds.

9. The St. Johns area contains trees typical of the Carolinian zone such as sassafras; tulip tree; black, pin, red, and white oak; black cherry; shag bark hickory; butternut; and flowering dogwood. Also found here are red and sugar maples, white pines, eastern hemlock, and American beeches. A large old beech tree is seen at this stop.

10. The trout pond contains not only trout, but also a variety of animal and plant life including common toads, spring peepers, flathead minnows, eastern painted turtles, and the green heron.

Three other well-marked trails lead off the Sassafras Stroll and are recommended for those who still have energy left or wish to linger longer in this delightful Carolinian forest setting:

Horseshoe Trail: 0.6 km (0.4 miles)
St. Johns Ridge: 1.7 km (1.1 miles)
Tulip Tree Trail: 1.7 km (1.1 miles)

Further Information

A 17-page brochure describing the birds, trees, ferns, and other natural delights of the Sassafras Stroll nature trail is available by calling or writing the Niagara Peninsula Conservation Authority (see Appendix). The Conservation Authority also offers brochures on other conservation areas in the region.

The Rainbow Trout: A Fish with Many Names (but not Wanda)

The rainbow trout has many noms de plume including the Kamloops trout, steelhead trout, coast rainbow trout, and silver trout. Originally native to the eastern Pacific Ocean and fresh waters west of the Rockies, it has now been introduced throughout North America. Stream residents are typically 30 to 45 cm (12 to 18 inches) long whereas those that live in the ocean or the Great Lakes are generally 50 to 76 cm (20 to 30 inches) in length. As its name indicates, the rainbow trout's colour can vary considerably. Mostly a bottom feeder, the rainbow trout eats a variety of invertebrates such as plankton, crustaceans, insects, snails, and leeches and fish eggs. Their life span is from three to eight years.

TOUR 3:
A Detailed Map of the Short Hills
(*Map 16*)

One of the most detailed maps in the Niagara region (1:10,000 scale with 5-metre contours) has been prepared of an area of the Short Hills that includes the Boy Scout Camp Wetaskiwin and part of Short Hills Provincial Park. This area is typical of both the Short Hills and the Niagara Escarpment and contains Carolinian forest, limestone crags, and waterfalls. The map can be used by anyone who is interested in cartography, map reading, or simply hiking away from the beaten path. The map was prepared by the Niagara Orienteering Club and is used for orienteering competitions, which are much like car rallying except done on foot with map and compass. The map may be purchased at the Scout Shop in St. Catharines (see Appendix).

Parking is available at Camp Wetaskiwin, located off Pelham Road a few miles southwest of St. Catharines. Be sure to register with the Camp custodian. An interesting outing is to visit Swayze's Falls, near the southern edge of the map.

Map 16, Orienteering map of the Short Hills

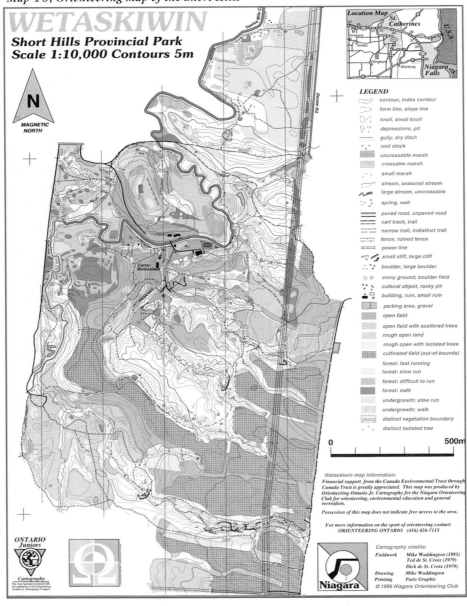

Chapter 11

GRAPE ESCAPES

A sampling of Niagara Wines

It seems only a decade ago that wine connoisseurs turned their noses up at even the mention of Niagara wines. But now that has all changed and Niagara vintages compete with the finest in the world. And the best part is that you can leisurely motor the backroads of Niagara, wending your way through orchards and vineyards from winery to winery, where you can sip Reislings, Gewurztraminers, Chardonnays, and Pinot Noirs. You won't be alone as wine touring has emerged as a popular pastime, offering a serene alternative to the usual crowded tourist meccas of Niagara Falls and Niagara-on-the-Lake. There's no finer way to see Niagara or to spend a summer afternoon.

What makes wine touring so pleasant is the charming boutique appearance of the wineries – they are a delight to visit, even aside from the free (or nominally-priced) wine sampling. The Niagara-on-the-Lake wineries were the first to attract tourists. Inniskillin, Château des Charmes, and Hillebrand not only make award winning wines, but visiting them is easy due to their proximity to the well-travelled Niagara Parkway.

The real sign of wine touring's coming of age, however, has been the remarkable growth of wineries west of the Welland Canal, away from the traditional tourist areas. Thirteen wineries are now located in the western group, many of which have only sprung up in the past few years. Combined with the ten wineries east of the Canal, there is a great selection, and it can take days and even weeks to discover the enchantment

Wine route sign

and individual personality of them all.

Vineland Estates, for example, has an attractive tasting centre and store, an 1855 carriage house for banquets, and a fashionable restaurant and wine bar, the WineDeck, which offers not only gourmet meals, but also glorious views of the vineyards. Hernder Estates has created a story-book setting by renovating an 130-year-old barn and building a pond and the only covered bridge in Niagara. One of the prettiest wineries is Walters Estates, which features a ski-style chalet with a central stone fireplace and wonderful vistas of rolling vineyards and Lake Ontario. It's a wonderfully soothing place to sit with a loved one or special friends, pondering some of life's imponderables over a glass of vintage wine.

Château des Charmes recently opened its new facility, styled after the magnificent châteaus of France's Bordeaux region. Cave Spring has created an entire tourist mecca around its winery, complete with an up-scale restaurant, luxury inn, antique stores, art shops, and more. What is particularly alluring is that every winery has its own distinctive character, and their styles vary from the modest operation to the spectacular.

The wineries also tempt you with entertainment. For example, Hillebrand Estates has bicycle tours of the surrounding vineyards and holds an annual jazz festival. Inniskillin's winery has an art gallery in the loft. Henry of Pelham offers Shakespearean plays on mid-summer nights. Hernder Estates has jazz on weekend evenings. The Tour de Vin, loosely based on the famous Tour de France, is staged by the eight Niagara-on-the-Lake wineries. The challenge is to visit each of the wineries preferably, but not necessarily, by bicycle, where you taste two selected vintages and get your passport stamped.

So why is Niagara one of the few places in Canada where quality grapes can grow? Although Canada is usually considered to be a land of snow and ice, the Niagara area is at its southernmost point and actually lies in the world's northern wine-growing belt, comparing favorably to other great wine regions. For example, Niagara is at the same latitude as the Rioja region of Spain and the Chianti Classico zone of Italy. In addition, the area has a unique microclimate influenced by Lakes Ontario and Erie and the Niagara Escarpment. The Niagara area has some of the most mineral-rich soil in the world, which produces not only great grapes but also bountiful crops of cherries, pears, apples, plums, and peaches. Roadside stands offer a cornucopia of freshly-picked fruit and vegetables at bargain prices.

Today, Niagara's wineries have become a major business success story. The Niagara region is particularly suited to producing very high quality Icewine, a rich dessert wine made from grapes that have frozen on the vine. Local wineries have won numerous international awards for this rich wine.

A sign-posted wine tour, developed by the wine industry, winds through this pastoral scenery. The wineries all

The Remaking of a Grape

The quality of Niagara wines has changed remarkably in the past decade. Originally, Niagara wines were based on the "labrusca grape", a native North American species. The "labrusca" grape has a very distinctive smell and flavour that, although suitable for sherries, is unappealing for table wines. Several wineries that specialized in sherries closed in the mid 1980s as the popularity of this drink diminished.

Attempts were made to grow European "vinifera" for wine but only met with limited success at first. Because the "labrusca" grape was remarkably resistant to soil diseases, horticulturists tried to cross breed European and American grape species. A significant number of these hybrids was produced, but they generally proved to be unpopular with the public. Later, techniques for grafting vinifera to North American rootstock were developed and subsequently formed the foundation for the present success of Niagara wines.

Large scale plantings of "viniferas" and "vinifera" hybrids, which include Pinot Noir, Cabernet Sauvignon, Cabernet Franc, Merlot, Gamay, Chardonnay, and Riesling, began in the 1980s.

provide guided tours and have reception areas where you can sample internationally acclaimed wines.

For purposes of touring, the wine region of Niagara can be divided into two parts. The eastern section (that is, east of the Welland Canal) is centered on Niagara-on-the-Lake and is perhaps the more interesting because several of the wineries are located close together so that you can visit them either by car or bicycle. The proximity of the Niagara Parkway offers many interesting side excursions and many lovely picnic sites.

A vintner checking his wares

VQA: Putting Quality in the Bottle

The bottles of most of the better wines of Niagara carry the symbol VQA on the label. These three letters stand for Vintners Quality Alliance and have been an important factor in achieving international recognition of Niagara wines. In a nutshell, the VQA designation assures the consumer of a quality wine. It means that the wine has been tasted and approved by an independent quality control panel and that the wine is made from 100% Ontario grapes of the type specified on the label. As Tony Aspler, the author of "Vintage Canada" stated, "The single most important factor in the advance in quality of Ontario wines has been the introduction of the VQA. This ... set the course for global recognition." Plans are afoot to expand the system to include an identification of different viticultural regions within Ontario.

The wineries west of the Canal are also attractive and well worth visiting; however, being more spread out, they are better suited to car tours. The historic town of Jordan is a convenient and picturesque staging area.

Within Niagara, there are subtle differences in character from area to area that are important to the wine connoisseur. The eastern wineries are located on the plain of an old glacial lake whereas some of the western wineries are on a terrace, or bench, of the ancient lake. Because of this, the two areas have different soils and microclimates. The net result is that the Niagara-on-the-Lake area is generally better known for red wines and the high terraces of the Vineland area for white wines such as Riesling. The vineyards next to Lake Ontario have a different character from those that are removed from its moderating influence.

Recognizing that food and wine go together like Bogey and Bacall, the wineries have been quietly getting into the eatery business. At the top end of the price scale are the Vineyard Café at Hillebrand Estates, On the Twenty Restaurant and Wine Bar at Cave Spring, and the WineDeck at Vineland Estates, which feature local cuisine and their own wines. Taking the edge off your hunger, however, does not need to make a major dent in the wallet. Even the smaller wineries are now catering to the famished and have cafés or picnic areas to offer, if not regular meals, at least special weekend barbecues.

TOUR 1:
Niagara-on-the-Lake Driving Tour
(Map 17)

This car tour of the eastern wineries follows the established wine tour route, as shown in Map 17. You can customize the tour to visit all or some of the following wineries, all of which offer wine sampling as well as boutiques. This tour, which passes delightful orchards, vineyards, and

The Exotic (and Expensive) Icewine
Icewine has rapidly gained an international reputation as the Cadillac of wines. And nowhere is it made better than here in Niagara. The grapes are left on the vine into early winter, usually until late December or early January. They are picked at night with the temperatures at -8°C so the grapes stay frozen. This temperature is critical because it freezes the water in the grape but not the inner nectar. The grape presses, which are usually moved outside to maintain the cold condition, gently squeeze the grapes as they are brought in from the field. Not much syrup emerges, but it is oh so rich! From this point on, the wine making proceeds as usual. Sadly, because of the small yield and the manual picking, the price is high. The small bottles (375 ml) into which icewine is placed reflects not only its high cost but also its rich and sweet flavour that is best enjoyed while lingering over dessert.

fields of roses and multicoloured flowers, demonstrates why this area is considered one of the most fertile in Canada.

Inniskillin winery

To provide some guidance to which vineyards you might wish to visit, we have ranked the wineries on a scale of 1 to 5, with 1 being the lowest score and 5 the highest. In other words, a winery with a higher number is deemed to be more interesting and more worthy of a visit than one with a lower score. Please note that this is a subjective ranking based on our experiences and taste. Further-more, the ranking does not take into account the quality of the wine.

1. Château des Charmes Wines, 1025 York Road. The winery is set in a magnificent, large château in an immaculate 34 hectare (85 acre) vineyard, which is reminiscent of the great wine growing areas of France. The Bosc family were amongst the first in Niagara to intro-duce vinifera and hybrid grapes [5].

Map 17, Niagara-on-the-Lake Winery Tour

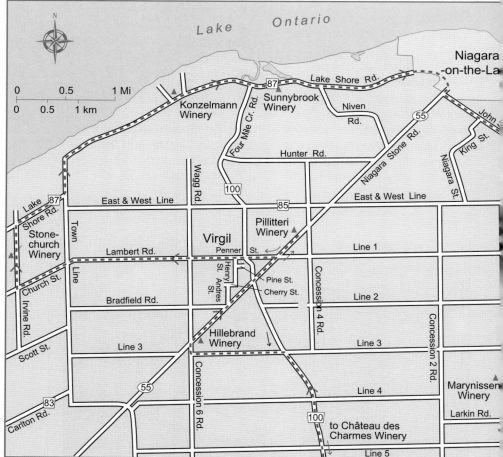

2.   Pillitteri Estates, 1696 Highway 55. This is a one-stop shopping winery centre, which also sells fruit, vegetables, flowers, and lip-smacking home baked breads and pies [3].

3.   Hillebrand Estates Winery, Highway 55 southwest of Virgil. One of the larger wineries in Ontario, Hillebrand offers bicycle tours of the surrounding vineyards and gourmet dining at the Vineyard Café. A popular jazz festival is held in the summer (see Chapter 17) [5].

4.   Stonechurch Vineyards, 1270 Irvine Road, takes its name from the oldest church in Niagara (circa 1853), which is located on the winery property. A family-run operation, they specialize in Icewine and friendly hospitality [4].

5.   Konzelmann Estate Winery, 1096 Lakeshore Road. The vineyards are set next to Lake Ontario and produce good Johannisberg Riesling-based wines [1].

6.   Sunnybrook Farm Estate Winery, 1425 Lakeshore Road. This is Ontario's only exclusive fruit (i.e. non-grape) winery. Started in 1993 as a supplement to farming, the winery has quickly gained a following for its peach, pear, apple and cherry wines [2].

7.   Reif Estate Winery, 15608 Niagara Parkway. With a lineage that boast thirteen generations of winemakers, it is not surprising that the Reifs are renowned for their quality wines. The winery also has a bed & breakfast, The Grand Victorian, in a magnificent century old mansion [3].

8.   Inniskillin Wines, Line 3 at Niagara Parkway. The unusual name derives from an Irish military regiment, the Inniskillin Fusiliers, who served here during the War of 1812. The tasting rooms are set in a picturesque restored barn with an art gallery in the loft. The winery offers a self-guided tour. Inniskillin was one of the first wineries to develop a reputation for Ontario wines based on the new vinifera and hybrid grapes [5].

9.   Marynissen Estates, Concession 1. A small, family-run operation, the focus is on red wines, particularly Cabernet Sauvignon [2].

10.   Vincor-Niagara Cellars, 4887 Dorchester Road, Niagara Falls. Vincor International is Canada's largest winery. It was a product of the merger of Brights and Cartier wineries; it also owns Inniskillin. Their premium wines are marketed under the Jackson Triggs label. The Sawmill Creek line has also become very popular [2].

The locations of eight of the above wineries are shown on Map 17, along with a suggested driving tour. Château des Charmes lies slightly to the south of the others and is shown on Map 12. Vincor-Niagara is geographically removed from the rest. To visit Vincor, proceed to Dorchester Road in Niagara Falls; the winery is located on the west side of the street about half way between Thorold Stone Road and Lundy's Lane.

Niagara-on-the-Lake vineyards

TOUR 2:
Cycling Tour of Niagara-on-the-Lake Wineries *(Map 17)*

A number of delightful bike tours can be organized around the Niagara-on-the-Lake wineries and the Niagara Parkway Recreational Trail. One of our favourites begins by finding a nice picnic spot on the Niagara Parkway anywhere between Lines 1 and 3. Leave the car there and bicycle to Inniskillin, Reif, and Marynissen wineries to sample their fine wares. The more energetic can also cycle to Pillitteri and Hillebrand wineries. We suggest that you purchase a chilled bottle of wine at one of the stops.

On returning to your parking site you can enjoy the wine over a picnic (don't forget a corkscrew!). Those who still have some energy left and wish to explore further can cycle north along the Recreational Trail into the Town of Niagara-on-the-Lake. We recommend a visit to the historic Olde Angel Inn to quench your thirst. Suggested tours of this charming Town are presented in Chapter 12.

Tour 3:
Driving Tour of Western Wineries *(Map 18)*

This car tour of the western wineries follows the established wine tour route, as shown in Map 18. Exit the Queen Elizabeth Way west of Grimsby at Fifty Road (exit 78) and the first stop, Andres Wines, is almost immediately on the South Service Road. Then join Highway 8, also known as Regional Road 81. Although the tour is posted with distinctive blue signs, be careful, as it is easy to miss some of the turnoffs.

You can customize your tour to visit all or some of the following wineries:

1. Andrés Wines, 697 South Service Road, Grimsby. The premium wines are sold under the label Peller Estates. The Peller family also operates wineries in British Columbia with outlets in five provinces [2].

2. Stoney Ridge Cellars, 1468 Highway 8, Winona. The winery, which also makes fruit wines, is associated with Puddicombe Farms with a country store that sells farm-made jellies and fresh baked goods. This is a family-oriented operation with a petting zoo for the children [3].

3. Kittling Ridge Estate Winery & Spirits, 297 South Service Road, Grimsby. This is the only winery in Canada that also makes spirits, including the unique Icewine & Brandy and a fascinating array of tropical drinks. It features the Casablanca Bistro Patio Bar and Grill [3].

4. Thirty Bench Winery, 4281 Mountainview Road, Beamsville. A small, newly-founded winery, it is located on the Beamsville Bench, an excellent grape growing area located on the rise leading up to the escarpment [1].

5. Walters Estates, 3999 Locust Lane, Beamsville. The winery is like a chalet set in a hillside, with decks overlooking glorious rolling vineyards. A large central fireplace makes this a wonderful visit in winter time [4].

6. Magnotta Cellars, 4701 Ontario Street, Beamsville. Magnotta

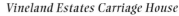

Vineland Estates Carriage House

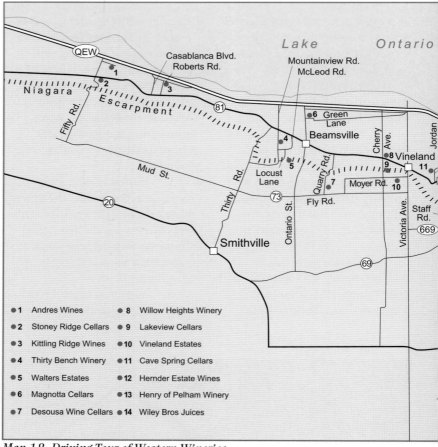

Map 18, Driving Tour of Western Wineries

offers good prices and has some different wines created by blending Ontario and imported wines. However, the outlet is a strip mall store [1].

7. DeSousa Wine Cellars, 3753 Quarry Road, Beamsville. Set in a red-tiled Mediterranean-style building, the winery features Portuguese wines, which are sold under the Dois Amigoes label. The boutique has three levels of decks, an 18th-century wine press from Portugal, and a picnic area [4].

8. Willow Heights Winery, 3751 Regional Road 81, Vineland. A small, newly-started operation, it specializes in Chardonnay, Pinot Noir, and Icewine. It hopes to soon release wine from Zinfandel and Syrah grapes [? – winery opened shortly after book went to press].

9. Lakeview Cellars Estate Winery, 4037 Cherry Avenue, south of Highway 8, Beamsville. This small winery is a family-run operation [2].

10. Vineland Estates Winery,

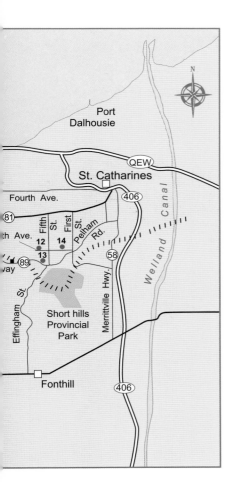

tures Niagara cuisine, and the luxurious Vintners Inn. The white wines, Riesling, Gewurztraminer, Chardonnay, and Icewine are highly regarded. You can also enjoy nearby antique stores, a museum, and art galleries [5].

12. Hernder Estate Wines, 1607 8th Avenue, St. Catharines. The winery is set in a story-book backdrop that is entered through the only covered bridge in Niagara. The winery and tasting rooms are in a fully restored 130-year-old Victorian barn, and the grounds include a wishing well, stone walls, and a pond with a fountain [4].

13. Henry of Pelham Family Estate Winery, 1469 Pelham Road, St. Catharines. In 1842, Henry Smith built the tavern that today houses the tasting and banquet rooms of Henry of Pelham and is operated by his descendants [3].

A pleasant surprise along the wine route is Wiley Brothers grape juice plant at 1175 8th Avenue at First Street, St. Catharines. This family farm has been run by the Wileys for six generations and has 140 hectares (350 acres) of grapes under cultivation producing 23 varieties. After the tour you can sample many exotic grape juices, which are never seen on supermarket shelves.

More Information

For more detailed information regarding the wines and wineries of Niagara, contact the individual wineries directly. Information may also be obtained from the Wine Council of Ontario (see Appendix).

3620 Moyer Road, Vineland. Vineland Estates has become one of the more successful, and picturesque, wineries in Niagara. It features a historic carriage house, circa 1857, which is used for banquets, a bed and breakfast cottage, a restaurant, and a glorious view from the licensed Winedeck [5].

11. Cave Spring Cellars, 3836 Main Street, Jordan. The winery is set in the historic town of Jordan and is complemented by the On-the-Twenty Restaurant and Wine Bar, which fea-

Chapter 12

NIAGARA-ON-THE-LAKE:
PRETTIEST TOWN IN CANADA

Stately mansion on John Street

During the War of 1812, Niagara-on-the-Lake came under fierce bombardment and was the scene of bloody battles. Today the town is still under seige, but by hordes of friendly tourists shooting cameras instead of muskets. And there is good reason for the ongoing invasion. Besides having the reputation as one of the prettiest towns in Canada, Niagara-on-the-Lake is also one of the most fascinating historically. The Town has retained its 19th century charm and

is a wonderful place to explore with its forts, grand mansions, colourful gardens and parks, and pot-pourri of arts and crafts.

Strategically situated at the mouth of the mighty Niagara River, Niagara-on-the-Lake played a key role in much of the early history of Upper Canada including early government, the War of 1812, commerce, and most recently as a centre for tourism and the arts. In fact, it is said that to understand the history of Niagara-on-the-Lake is to understand the history of early Ontario.

The settlement was originally known as Butlersburg, in honour of Colonel John Butler, the commander of Butler's Rangers. The Town received official status in 1781 when it became known as Newark, a British military site and haven for British Loyalists fleeing the United States in the volatile aftermath of the American Revolution. Later, it changed names again, this time to Niagara.

Niagara was named the first capital of Upper Canada (now the province of Ontario), and the first provincial parliament was convened at Navy Hall in 1792 by Lieutenant-Governor John Graves Simcoe. During the War of 1812, the capital was moved to York (later to be renamed as Toronto) so as to be farther from the areas of combat.

The Town played a central part in the War of 1812. It was taken by American forces after a two day bombardment by cannons from Fort Niagara and the American fleet, followed by a bloody battle. Later in the war, the Town was razed and burnt to the ground by American soldiers as they withdrew to Fort Niagara. Undaunted by this setback, the citizens rebuilt the Town after the War, with the residential quarter around Queen Street and toward King Street, where the new Court House was rebuilt out of firing range of the cannons of Fort Niagara.

In the 1880s, the Town was renamed as Niagara-on-the-Lake to avoid confusion with Niagara Falls. The central part is referred to as Old Town or Old Niagara.

Please note that the directions in the following tours refer to "map north" as shown on Map 19, not to true north.

> **Niagara-on-the-Lake is a town of firsts.** *The first census in Canada was held here in 1782. The first grist mill was built in 1783. The first legislature of Upper Canada was convened here in 1792.*

TOUR 1:
Overview of the Town (Map 19)

This tour is well suited for bicycling as it is relatively long, although intrepid walkers will also enjoy it. If bicycling, allow about two hours and if walking, allow about three to four hours for this wonderful insight into the history of Canada. Please refer to Map 19; the numbers on the map correspond to the numbers in the following text.

The starting point is Navy Hall (1) on the River Road below Fort George, which has free parking. Take a moment to go out on the dock for a view of the Niagara River, which in the summer time is abuzz with sail and power boats. Across the river is Fort Niagara.

Navy Hall was built in 1775-1787 for the use by officers of the Navy Department serving on Lake Ontario. In 1792, it was selected by Governor Simcoe as the site for the first Parliament of Upper Canada. Later, it was moved here from its original location at the top of Front Street. Navy Hall was restored in 1911 and used by the Military Camp

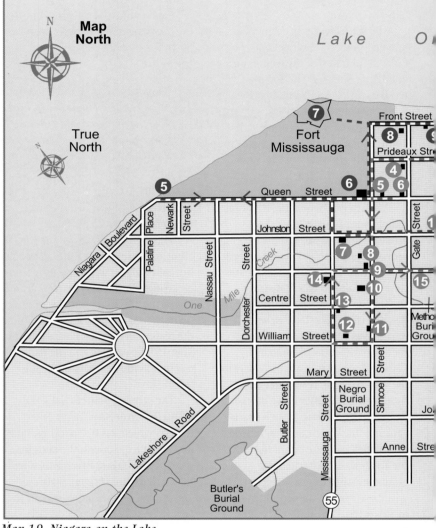

Map 19, Niagara-on-the-Lake

during the First World War. Further restored by the Niagara Parks Commission, it now serves as a military museum.

Proceed south keeping the river on your left. In less than a kilometre (0.6 miles), turn left onto the Niagara River Recreational Pathway (the bike path) which parallels the road and proceed to the first carpark where you turn right and rejoin the road. Cross Queens Parade and proceed west along John Street. Soon on the left you will see four mansions set in large mani-

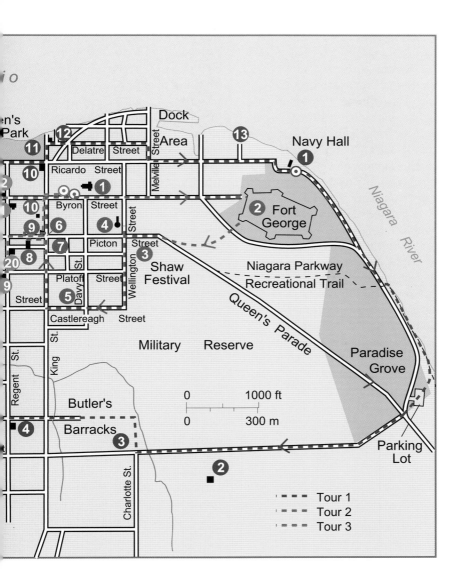

cured grounds and surrounded by ivy covered stone walls. The second estate at 120 John Street is Randwood (2), the former Niagara Institute, a well known conference centre.

Turn right opposite the corner of Charlotte Street at the distinctive

brown and yellow sign announcing Butler's Barracks (3). This large area was set aside as a military reserve at the time of the Loyalists arriving from America. After the destruction of Fort George, the British constructed Fort Mississauga and also established new barracks here, well beyond the range of the cannons at Fort Niagara. Proceed about 50 metres and turn left between two rows of trees passing just to the left of three old cannons. There is no path here today, but it was once a camp road that has felt the marching rhythm of thousands of military boots. Proceed past the cannons and the old ordnance gun sheds.

Continue straight ahead crossing King Street and proceed along Mary Street. Note the Miller- Taylor House (4) on the southeast corner of Mary and Regent Streets (46 Mary Street), which was built in 1817 and features seven fireplaces. Turn right onto Victoria and then left on Johnson. You are now in the Old Town and there are many interesting old homes dating from the early 1800s. The intersection of Victoria and Johnson Streets has three noteworthy houses; please refer to stops (16), (17), and (18) in Tour 3.

Turn right on Mississauga Street and left on Queen Street. As you proceed along Queen, take time to inspect and enjoy the wonderful homes on the left. Many of these mansions were built recently, but they have maintained the Victorian style of the Old Town. The golf course is on the right. At the end of Queen Street, a stone cairn (5) commemorating the Battle of Fort George is located on the lake side. Look for a small gravestone to the east of the cairn, which marks the spot where the bodies of three soldiers from the Battle of 1813 were found in 1899.

Return along Queen Street and turn left on Simcoe Street. Note the Kiely House (6) at 209 Queen Street, on the northwest corner, built in 1832 and recently converted to a restaurant and inn. The original symmetrical Georgian design has been altered by renovations. From the corner of Simcoe and Front Streets look west to see Fort Mississauga (7) which now forms an integral part of the golf course. It is permissable to cross the golf course and visit the fort, but be courteous and watch out for low-flying golf balls.

Fort Mississauga was built in great panic in 1814 to replace Fort George after it was destroyed by the retreating American forces in 1813. The Fort was placed out of reach of the guns of Fort Niagara on the site of the first lighthouse on the Great Lakes (1804). Constructed from rubble from the ruins of the town; the cornerstone has a foundation stone from the lighthouse. It was the first and only fort erected in North America after the modern five-pointed star fort system in Europe. Fortunately, the much-feared second invasion by American forces never materialized, and today the fort's ramparts, which have not been restored, enclose one of the nine holes of the golf course. The only bombardment that the fort's walls have endured are the carom of errant golfballs.

Proceed along Front Street passing the Oban Inn (8) on the right. The original Oban Inn was built in 1842 and was once the home of Duncan Malloy, a retired sea captain from Oban, Scotland. The Inn was destroyed by fire on Christmas Eve, 1994, during dinner. The Inn was expertly restored with items salvaged from the fire, and, with additional fire precautions, the Inn served Christmas Eve dinner to the same group of guests one year later. There are dining rooms and a terrace on the main floor, as well as Shaw's Corner, whose walls are lined with auto-graphed photographs of Shaw Festival actors and actresses.

Next you pass William Kirby's House (9) at 130 Front Street, which was built in 1818 and is marked by an historic plaque, and the Old Bank House (10) at 10 Front Street, which was built in 1817 and was formerly the Bank of Upper Canada when this part of Town was the commercial area, but now has been converted to a bed and breakfast establishment. The pleasant Queen's Royal Park (11) contains a gazebo and offers wonderful panoramas of Fort Niagara and Lake Ontario. The park was the original site of the Queen's Royal Hotel (1869), the most prestigious hotel in Niagara, which was dismantled during the depression. The gazebo was added in 1983 for the filming of the movie "The Dead Zone." On a clear day, the skyscrapers of Toronto can be seen shimmering on the horizon.

Turn left on King Street and right on Delatre Street. Note the Whale Inn (12) at 66 King Street, built about 1835, on the corner. The wing on the lower level was particularly conve-nient for sailors when it was origi-nally a tavern; they could beach their crafts on the shore and saunter in for

a dram. Turn right on Melville and left on Ricardo Street. The Pump House Art Centre (13) at 245 Ricardo is well worth a stop with its adjoining cottage, lighthouse, and riverside gazebo. Proceed along Ricardo and you will soon be back at Navy Hall.

The next two tours explore the Town in more detail with Tour 2 looking at "establishments" such as museums, churches, and the Shaw Festival, while Tour 3 focuses on the gracious old homes of the 1800s. Both tours start at the same place (north side of Simcoe Park) and each forms a loop. The two tours can be done individually, or for the lover of long walks, they can be combined to form a single "figure of 8" tour.

TOUR 2:
The "Establishments" of Niagara-on-the-Lake (Map 19)

This walk starts from the north side of Simcoe Park, where there is usually ample free parking, except at peak summer tourist times. The walk itself will take about one hour; how-ever, there are many interesting stops that can easily add several more hours. The walk explores, with a small detour, the areas to the east of King Street. Please refer to Map 19; the numbers on the map correspond to the numbers in the following text.

Start by crossing to the north side of Byron Street to St. Mark's Church (1), which was originally built between 1804 - 1809. Used as a hos-pital during the War of 1812, this Anglican church was burned by the retreating American soldiers in 1813 but was rebuilt by 1822. The oldest library in Upper Canada (now Ontario) is in the Rectory with books dating from the 16th century. The churchyard of St. Mark's was the earliest burial ground in the town, and contains may fascinating tombstones from the early nineteenth century.

Proceed east along Byron Street to Fort George (2). The wooden palisades look remarkably frail in contrast to the sturdy stone walls and buttresses of the rival Fort Niagara on the American side of the river. Built by the British between 1796 and 1799 to guard the entrance to the Niagara · River, Fort George played a strategic role in the War of 1812 and was used by General Isaac Brock as the base for British military operations in the area. The fort was overrun and burned by the Americans in May 1813. More than a century later during the Great Depression, the fort was restored to the original specifications of the Royal Engineers as a make-work project. All 11 of the original 14 buildings restored are furnished as they were from 1797 to 1813; all hardware used in the restoration was made by hand at Fort George in the Artificer's Shop. It is particularly delightful to visit the Fort on Canada Day or other special occasions when the sound of muskets and the smell of gunpowder are heavy in the air as battles of the War of 1812 are re-enacted by townsfolk in period costumes.

Walk back toward Town along Queens Parade until you reach the Shaw Festival Theatre (3), which is on the left. Begun in 1962, the Shaw Festival has gained an international reputation for excellence. Plays by George Bernard Shaw and his contemporaries are presented each season from April until October. The theatre was built in 1972 to accommodate the intense demand for tickets that caused it to outgrow the tiny Court House Theatre, where it began.

Continue toward Town and at Wellington Street, cross over and visit St. Vincent de Paul Church (4). The oldest part of the church was completed in 1834. The first catholic mass was celebrated in Niagara-on-the-Lake in 1669. The church was renovated in 1890 and again in 1964.

Cross back over Picton Street and continue south along Wellington, turning right when it ends at Castlereagh Street. Soon on the right is the Niagara Historical Society Museum (5). Founded in 1895 and housing over 20,000 artifacts, this structure was the first in Ontario to be built solely as a museum.

Continue along Castlereagh Street to King Street and turn right. At Queen Street make a left turn keeping on the left side of Queen Street. At the intersection take a moment to admire the Clock Tower (6), which was erected as a memorial to the soldiers who lost their lives in the First World War and provides the focal point of the main street. On the southeast corner is the Prince of Wales Hotel (7), which was built in 1880.

At 26 Queen Street is the Court House (8), which was built in 1847 on the site of the Government House (1792). It has one of the oldest town bells in Canada, which has rung continuously on the hour since March 27, 1839. Not used for judicial purposes since 1862 when the county seat was moved to St. Catharines, the Court House was the original home of the Shaw Festival and is still used as a venue for plays.

Cross over Queen Street and return on the other side. The Niagara Apothecary (9) is located at 5 Queen Street. Built in 1819, this building served continuously as a pharmacy, dispensing remedies and cures to the ill until 1971 when it received a major facelift and was converted to a museum. It has the honour of being the longest operating pharmacy in Ontario. Much of the original apothecary-ware has been re-acquired, including patent medicines, leech containers, and cure-all tonics that promise to alleviate tooth ache, cholera, indigestion, rheumatism, gout, diarrhea, and many other maladies. Original fixtures such as black walnut counters and crystal chandeliers are a contrast to the sterile interiors of modern super drug stores.

Turn left at King Street and proceed to 177 King Street, the Preservation Fine Art Gallery (10), a delightfully restored Victorian mansion, which houses work by the popular local artists Trisha Romance, Alex Colville, and Philip Craig. The house alone makes a visit worthwhile.

Across the street is Simcoe Park with tall and elegant shade trees under which you can rest, perhaps enjoying a picnic, while you recover from your walk.

Soldier and cannon on guard at Fort George

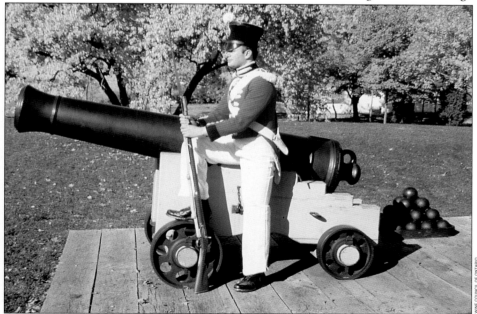

WINE COUNCIL OF ONTARIO

TOUR 3:

The Gracious Homes of Niagara-on-the-Lake *(Map 19)*

This walk passes along sedate tree-lined residential streets with gracious homes that reflect the charm of the early 1800s. This walk, which takes about 1.5 hours, starts from the north side of Simcoe Park where there is usually ample free parking, except at peak summer tourist times.

Cross King Street and proceed west along Prideaux Street. Although the homes along this street are of different styles and ages, they all exude a quiet elegance and charm. On the left at 42 Prideaux Street, just before Regent Street, is the Stewart-McLeod House (1), built in the early 1820s for a local lawyer. It contains one of the finest spiral staircases of that period.

Past Regent Street on the right is the Promenade House (2) at 55 Prideaux Street, which was built about 1820 and was an hotel in Victorian times, although it has been a private residence for many years.

The large brick house, Demeath (3) at 69 Prideaux Street, was built right after the end of the War of 1812 on a previous foundation. It was the home of Dr. Robert Kerr, and it is believed that his office was also in this house.

On the left, on the other side at 155 Gate Street, is a large buff-coloured house. This building was originally constructed in the late 1820s as a Methodist meeting-house (4) at a location about three blocks away. It was later sold and moved to the present location.

Turn left at Simcoe Street with

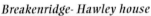
Breakenridge- Hawley house

views onto the golf course and proceed past Kiely House on the right (refer to stop (6) of tour 2). Turn left and go east along Queen street. On your left at 187 Queen Street, note the Crysler-Rigg House (5), which was built in about 1822. This substantial wooden house is of a three-bay design. The attractive verandah at the back was added at about the turn of the century. At 157 Queen Street is the Rogers-Blake-Harrison House (6), which was built circa 1823. The asymmetrical building is finished in stucco to imitate cut stone. Note the doorway with sidelights and fanlight. Today it is operated as a bed and breakfast. Retrace your steps back along Queen Street to Simcoe Street, turn left, and proceed southwards.

Make a small detour to the west to 234 Johnson Street to view the Clench House (7). Built immediately after the War of 1812, this is one of the finest properties in Niagara-on-the-Lake and occupies a 0.8 hectare (two acre) lot through which One Mile Creek quietly meanders.

Return along Johnson Street and turn right at Simcoe Street. On the right at 275 Simcoe Street is the Butler House (8), a small bungalow sitting well back on its lot. This 1817 house, once a derelict, was moved here and restored to its present condition. It features a kitchen in the basement with a dumb-waiter serving the dining room on the main level.

The Lockhart-Moogk House (9) at 289 Simcoe Street is next on the right. Dating from the post- 1812 period, it is a two-storey structure

Blain-Lansing House, 95 Johnston Street

with stucco covering brick.

Crossing Gage, next on the right, are Kirk Hall and St. Andrew's Presbyterian Church (10). Kirk Hall was originally an army hut that was brought here and renovated with brick cladding. The first church, built in 1794, was destroyed during the War of 1812. The present church rose in 1831 and has not changed significantly since then. The frontal facade is considered to be one of the finest examples of Greek Revival architecture in Ontario.

Creen House (11) at 363 Simcoe Street, on the right across Centre

Street, was originally built about 1820. Having fallen badly into disrepair, it was completely reconstructed about a decade ago with considerable attention to maintaining its original detail. It is fashionable in this part of Town to build houses that have the appearance of the 1800s. One of these is located next door to the Creen house, and you will notice many more during your walk.

Turn right on William and again on Mississauga Street. On the corner is the Breakenridge- Hawley House (12) at 392 Mississauga Street, which was built in 1818 and was John Breakenridge's second house. At the back is a separate coach house with three carriage bays and living quarters above. This house features one of the finest doorways of the Town's older homes.

Farther along Mississauga Street, facing Centre Street, is the Breakenridge-Ure House (13) at 240 Centre Street, John Breakenridge's third home. Built in 1823, it has nine fireplaces and a bake oven. On the left side, on the corner of Gage Street at 307 Mississauga Street, is the large clapboard Camp-Thompson House (14), which was built in 1818 and formerly was a private school.

Turn right and proceed along Gage Street. Immediately across Gate Street, on the right, is a row of evergreens enclosing the Methodist cemetery (15), which dates to about 1825. You passed the meeting house that once stood beside this cemetery earlier in the walk (stop 4).

Turn left on Victoria Street and proceed to the corner of Johnson

Street. There are three houses of note near this intersection. On the northwest corner at 105 Johnson Street is the Varey House (16), a large well-kept two-storey house that was built in 1837; it has a lean-to addition.

On the northeast corner at 95 Johnson Street stands the brick Blain-Lansing House (17). The date of construction, 1835, is shown in the keystone above the door. Formerly, the postman lived here, and the difference in bricks that were used to fill the entrance to his office is visible at the corner.

On the southeast corner at 96 Johnson Street is the Vanderlip-Marcy House (18). At one time this home, built in 1816, boasted a small front porch, which was moved to another house when the sidewalk was installed.

Proceed east along Johnson to Regent Street. On the southwest corner at 58 Johnson Street stands the Eckersley House (19), built in 1833 with its chimneys placed in the interior rather than on the exterior walls.

Turn north on Regent Street and proceed to the Olde Angel Inn (20) at number 224. Established in 1823 as the Harmonious Coach House, it boasts not only being the oldest inn in the Town but also a resident ghost, Captain John Swayze, who died in the War of 1812. This is one of our favorite pubs, and we recommend that you stop here to replenish your strength after this long stroll.

Proceed north along Regent to Queen Street. Turn right and then left on King Street to return to the starting point.

Chapter 13

CITY SCAPES

Welland Mural, "Upbound at Midnight"

Urban landscapes are, in their own way, as fascinating as natural beauties. Instead of a look at forest and dale, they provide an insight into the minds of the inhabitants. We can see, and enjoy, their characters, their way of life, and their social imprint. In this chapter we explore two cities in the Niagara Peninsula of Ontario. The first is Welland, a largely industrial city, which came into being because of the Welland Canal. The second is Port Dalhousie, a northern suburb of St. Catharines, Ontario. A child of the early Welland Canals, it was orphaned when the third

Welland Canal bypassed it. Although now a tourist centre, Port Dalhousie still retains its charming historical identity.

TOUR 1:
The Giant Murals of Welland
(Map 20)

The City of Welland, long associated with the Welland Canal, is gaining a reputation as the largest open-air art gallery in the world – and the canvasses are gigantic, stretching up to 25 metres (80 feet) long and three storeys high. To beautify the city, Welland commissioned

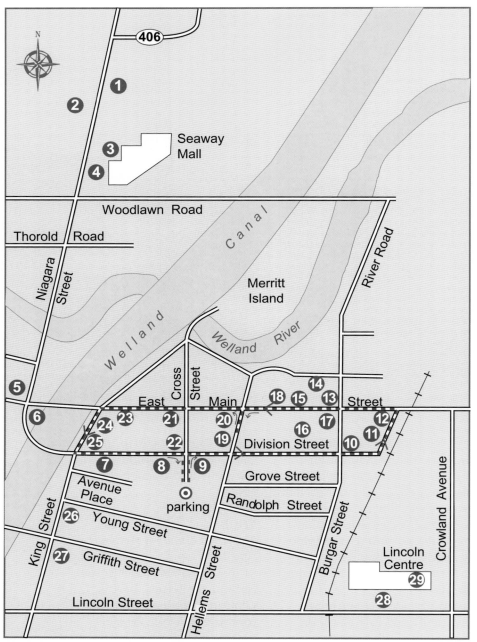

Map 20, The Giant Murals of Welland

artists from across Canada to paint murals on the sides of buildings. More than two dozen permanent, colourful murals depicting historical themes of the region now grace the city, adding a rich visual element to the urban landscape. Started in 1986, this is an ongoing project with new murals being added periodically.

Map 20 shows the locations of the murals and is keyed to the listing below. If you wish to see all the murals you will need to drive; however, as most of them are concentrated in the downtown area, a walking tour is an attractive option that will let you enjoy the giant art and also have a glimpse into the life of a city on the canal. A suggested tour is outlined on the map.

1. "Towpaths" at 1030 Niagara Street North, by Ross Beard, depicts a sailing ship being pulled through the Canal in the 1800s.

2. "Welland Dairies" at 871 Niagara Street North, by Mike Svob, has three panels showing the milk business in the early 1900s.

3. "History of the Niagara Peninsula" at 800 Niagara Street North on the Sears building at the Seaway Mall. This mural depicts the cultural and economic development of the Niagara Peninsula.

4. "History of the Welland Canal" at 800 Niagara Street North, on the front of the Seaway Mall. The artist captures the many obstacles that had to be overcome in the construction and development of the canal.

5. "Welland Trolley" at 1 Niagara Street, by David More. The NS&T trolley brought visitors to the

Welland County Fair on Denistoun Street from 1910 to 1930.

6. "Lift Bridges" at 31 West Main Street facing Niagara Street. Painted by Greg Garand, it depicts the canal prior to the completion of the by-pass to the east, when ships from around the world passed through the heart of the city.

7. "Welland's World War 1 Efforts," at 51 Division Street on Columbus Hall, by Risto Turunen, illustrates Welland's involvement in World War 1.

8. "New World" at 77 Division Street is a brick mosaic mural designed by Dutch artist Bas Degroot. The mural depicts people moving to a "New World" and can be interpreted from a spiritual or secular viewpoint.

9. "Three Historical Scenes" at 115 Division Street is by Toronto artist John Hood. It consists of three panels each containing a great deal of historical detail.

10. "Wagons" at 250 Division Street, by Andrew Miles. This is a stained-glass effect of several turn-of-the-century wagons and buggies.

11. "Education" at 285 East Main Street, by Risto Turunen. Teacher, principal, students, and school are based on old photographs.

12. "Triathlon" at 285 East Main Street, by Paul Elliot. The runner, cyclist, and swimmer are captured in a scene from the annual Welland Mike Burwell Triathlon.

13. "Upbound at Midnight" at 228 East Main Street, by Ross Beard. This is a night scene of a ship travelling south towards Port Colborne along the Welland Canal.

14. "Welland Fair" at 228 East Main Street, by John Hood. Three scenes from the 1940, 1958, and 1975 Welland Fair are shown.

15. "The Cordage Community" at 212 East Main Street, by Marsha Charlebois, depicts the employees of the Plymouth Cordage Company circa 1906 at work and play.

16. "Tell me about the Olden Days" a free-standing wall across the street from 212 East Main is by Chemainus, B.C. artist Dan Sawatzky. It depicts the arrival of immigrants in Welland circa 1910.

17. "Little Helper" at 225 East Main Street is also by Dan Sawatzky and depicts a farm family of father, son and grandson in a local agricultural scene.

18. "The Pond – New Year's Eve" at 188 East Main Street, by Ross Beard, depicts the Welland Junction area about 1970, with upturned earth suggesting the construction of the new canal by-pass.

19. "The Welland Club" at the corner of Hellems Avenue and East Main Street, by John Hood, depicts the professional club around 1920, with the Union Jack and lawn bowling featured prominently.

20. "Where Water Meets Rail" at 147 East Main Street, by Lorraine Coakley-Black, concentrates on various means of transportation.

21. "Tugboats" at 77 East Main Street, by Stefan Bell, depicts the tugboat "Hector" circa 1920, pulling barges and ships through the canal. Look for the artist's juggling equipment hidden in the mural.

22. "Steam Engine" on the side of the Bell Building on Cross Street, by Ron Baird, depicting the old "work horse" used in the construction of the old canals.

23. "Working Women" at 27 East Main Street, by Ted Zeigler, shows the contribution of women to the industrial work force in the factories of Welland.

24. "Downtown Welland" at 14 King Street, by Phillip Woolf, depicts the commercial life of early Welland.

25. "Main Street" at 22 King Street, by Mike Svob, contains two scenes of commercial activity in early downtown Welland.

26. "Canal Construction" at 140 King Street, by Bas Degroot, depicts the construction of the canal bypass.

27. "Canal Digging" at 175 King Street, by Brian Romagnoli, depicts the era around 1824, with great detail in six historic scenes.

28. "Paint by Number Mural" at 300 Lincoln Street East is the world's largest paint by number mural, completed by approximately 1,000 people. It depicts the diverse ethnic mixture that played a major role in Welland's development.

29. "O Canada," a relief Mural in Basswood, at 300 Lincoln Street East (inside the Lincoln Centre) by the Niagara Woodcarvers Association. This carving depicts the flora, fauna, and heraldry from countries of Europe and Asia, which are the homelands of a large percentage of the population of Welland. The birds and animals from these countries have come to the "Canadian Beaver Pond" to drink in peace and harmony.

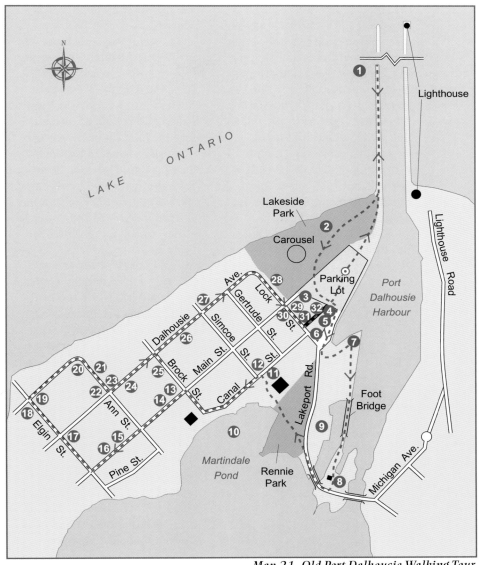

Map 21, Old Port Dalhousie Walking Tour

TOUR 2:
Old Port Dalhousie Walking Tour
(Map 21)

This is a wonderful walk that includes lighthouses, insights into the early history of the Welland

Canal, stately homes, and waterfront cafés.

Originally farmland, Port Dalhousie became a thriving maritime community at the northern entrance to the first three Welland Canals. At the turn of the century, so many ships passed this way that it was said that a person could cross the canal by jumping from deck to deck amidst a forest of masts. Port Dalhousie was incorporated as a Village in 1862 and was amalgamated with the growing City of St. Catharines in 1961. It fell into decline after being bypassed by the fourth canal. Today it is again flourishing, but as a lively tourist area with many restaurants and colourful boutiques displaying arts and crafts.

This walking tour begins at Lakeside Park which is located at the end of Lakeport Road and has ample free parking. The route is outlined in Map 21.

1. Port Dalhousie Piers. The two piers were built in 1838 to provide a more direct entrance to the Second Welland Canal than those serving the first Canal, which took an L-shaped route through what is now Lakeside Park. The piers, especially the western one, are a favorite spot for a quiet stroll to watch the sunset. The outer lighthouse on the eastern pier was built in 1879, and the inner one was built in 1898 to replace an earlier one that was destroyed by lightning.

2. Lakeside Park. This park, once the swampy, mosquito-infested mouth of Twelve Mile Creek, was filled with the soil from digging the canals. Its heyday was in the first half of this century when it operated as an immensely popular amusement park, including a merry-go-round, waterslide, and dance pavilion. In 1929, for example, nearly 300,000 people visited the Park, many coming from Toronto aboard the passenger ships "Dalhousie City" and "Northumberland." One of the few relics of its former glory is the wooden merry-go-round, which is famous for its 5-cent rides. Built in 1898 in Rhode Island, the merry-go-round was restored and installed at this spot in the 1970s by local residents, with the condition that a ride would cost a nickel in perpetuity.

3. Port Dalhousie Jail. Built in 1845, this is one of the smallest and oldest former jails remaining in Canada. It is a designated historical building.

Port Dalhousie piers

4. Port Mansion, 12 Lakeport Road. The building was constructed in 1860 and, due to its strategic location, has always been used as an hotel. In earlier days it was known as Houston's Hotel and the Union House. On summer days there is live entertainment on the patio, a great spot to people-watch and catch cool lake breezes.

5. 26 Lakeport Road. This bookstore, built in 1862, is one of the oldest buildings in the core area. It once operated as the NonSuch Hotel and is reported to have been the site of the first bowling alley in Port.

6. Murphy Building, 38 Lakeport Road on the corner. After a series of fires at the site, Edward Murphy constructed this building on the busiest corner of Port in 1885, establishing a ship's chandlery. In the early 1900s, the Back Club was a popular place for the well-to-do to gather and exchange news. It is now Murphy's Restaurant.

7. Lockhart Point Park. The centrepiece of this pretty little park is Lock One of the second Welland Canal. Note the fine stone work that, even after 150 years, is still in good condition.

Continue east through the park and turn right when you reach the waterway. Continue along and cross over the footbridge, which was constructed in 1996.

8. Locktender's Shanty. This small edifice is the last remaining Locktender's shanty of the third Welland Canal. Built in 1887, it was used to record the number of ships passing through the canal and to col-

lect fees. Cross over Lakeport Road and turn right and go back toward Port Dalhousie. Turn left into Rennie Park.

9. Lincoln Fabrics, 63 Lakeport Road. Built in 1900 by the Maple Leaf Rubber Company, this large industrial building was positioned here to take advantage of the transportation and power offered by the Canal. Originally, a second similar building was located across the road.

10. Royal Canadian Henley Regatta Course. Martindale Pond was the site of the first annual regatta in 1903. The grandstand was built in 1931 and can seat 2,000 people. Modeled after the famous Royal Henley Regatta in England, the Henley has grown to be the largest annual regatta in North America, attracting rowers from around the world.

Continue through the park and walk to the left of the Dalhousie House Seniors building, which was built in 1850 and was once part of the Muir Brothers drydocks, and go up the metal stairs.

11. 27 Canal Street. This two-storey home built circa 1840 displays elements of Georgian design.

12. 30 Canal Street. This house was built in 1875 by Johnson Gregory, Port Dalhousie's first postmaster. It features a prominent verandah, wooden trellis, and gingerbread trim.

13. 50 Main Street. Constructed in 1894, this Italianate style building now houses a store on the ground floor and apartment above.

14. 54 Main Street. Built in 1838, this one-storey house is thought to be the one of the oldest remaining buildings in Port. It was home to Captain John Reid, one of the first settlers to have lived in Port Dalhousie.

15. St. John's Anglican Church. Built in 1868, this is the oldest church in Port Dalhousie. It has a lovely bell tower topped by a weather vane. Its cemetery is located at 320 Main Street and contains the graves of many of Port's prominent early families.

16. St. Andrew's United Church. Built in 1894, St. Andrew's displays gothic influences in the windows on the front facade. The cemetery is located at the foot of Johnson Street.

17. St. Mary's Star of the Sea Roman Catholic Church. This gothic-styled church was completed in 1875 and used stones that were bought from Kingston as ballast on ships. The original steeple, which was tall enough to be seen from ships on the lake, blew over during a storm.

18. 31-35 Elgin Street. This building, originally located at 116 Dalhousie Avenue, was constructed in 1870 and served as Port's second school. It is now a triplex.

19. 27 Bayview Drive, on the corner. Built circa 1867, this ivy-covered building is one portion of the original St. John's rectory.

At the end of Bayview Drive where it meets Ann Street, there is a tiny park with two benches where you can rest and, on a clear day, see the skyline of Toronto across the lake.

20. 43 Ann Street on the right-hand corner. This 2 1/2 storey house

with a dormer was built circa 1865 by William Muir, one of the founders of Muir Brothers Dry Docks and Ship-yards. Originally a small frame house, it has undergone many renovations over the years.

21. 40 Ann Street on the left side. This two-storey English style, ivy covered house has wonderful views across the lake towards Toronto.

22. 88 Dalhousie Avenue, on the corner. This brick house was built in 1865 by David Muir, another of the founders of Muir Brothers Dry Docks and Shipyards.

23. 82 Dalhousie Avenue. This is the other portion of St. John's rectory. The prominent lantern that sits atop the roof is a "widow's walk" where the wives of sailors would look out onto the lake waiting the return of their husbands.

24. 75 Dalhousie Avenue. This saltbox-style white clapboard home was built in 1840 as a tailor shop on Main Street. It was moved to this site in 1860 and has an addition at the back.

25. Public Library, 23 Brock Street. This structure with a small bell-tower was built in 1863 by the Good Templars, who tended to the welfare of the community. The building served as the Town Hall until the amalgamation with St. Catharines in 1961.

26. 47 Dalhousie Avenue. The garage for this house is a renovated coach house topped by a lovely weathervane. The pulley to the hayloft door remains hanging from the brace.

Port Dalhousie garage with hayloft door and pulley

27. The Breakers, 30 Dalhousie Avenue. This large, white Italianate-style house was built in the 1880s. Moulded architectural detailing is found throughout the home. It has beautifully landscaped grounds surrounded by a white picket fence.

Continue along Dalhousie Street until it meets Lock Street and turn right.

28. 36 Lock Street. Built in 1845 as the Customs House, it also served as the harbourmaster's home. The harbourmaster collected duties and fines from the ships that passed through the canal. The building now houses numerous apartments.

Continue along Lock Street and cross Main Street.

29. Lakeside Hotel. Known as the Austin House when it was built in the 1890s, this three- storey, red brick building is of Italianate style. Note the four recessed bays on the facade which are each of different size.

30. Lion Tavern. Built in 1877 as the Wellington House, the window shapes and cornice features display a strong Italianate influence.

31. St. Catharines Craft Guild, 12 Lock Street. This structure was built in 1896 and served as a post office and grocery store. The wooden spindles, balustrade, and fan brackets which decorate the front facade are true to the original building.

32. Hogan's Alley. This alley has become a popular tourist walkway with its cafés and restaurants, but in the 1800s it was home to local roustabouts, and later it was a popular toboganning hill.

Chapter 14

BICYCLE TOURS:
SIX LOOKS AT NIAGARA

Cycling in Niagara

The bicycle is a wonderful invention. At a modest cost and with minimal upkeep, it offers the perfect form of transportation. Certainly, there is no better way to study a landscape than meandering at your own pace, vision unimpeded by the glare of a windscreen, free to roll along wherever your heart and impulses carry you. This chapter presents six bicycle tours that wend their way along country roads and give an insight into different parts of Niagara.

If you would like more information on these or other bike tours, contact the Niagara Freewheelers Bicycle Touring Club (see Appendix) who contributed most of these tours and hold weekly rides.

All six tours are circle routes so you can pick any convenient place to start and finish, instead of the starting places that are suggested.

TOUR 1:

Niagara-on-the-Lake *(Map 22)*

This pleasant, flat ride of about 23 kilometres (14 miles) takes you along the Niagara Parkway and into the rich fruit lands of Niagara-on-the-Lake. The suggested starting place is the parking lot of Fort George.

Head south along the Niagara Parkway recreational trail. At Line 1, turn west. The rest of the route, as shown on Map 22, is easy to follow except through Virgil. As you enter the town of Virgil heading east along Line 2, take the following streets through the town:

➤ turn left on Andres Street
➤ turn right on Cherry Street
➤ turn left on Henry Street
➤ turn right on Line 1 (Penner Street)
➤ turn right on Four-Mile Creek Road and take a coffee break at Silks Restaurant or the Donut Diner
➤ After coffee, back-track to Line 1
➤ turn right on East-West Line and proceed as shown on Map 22.

This tour can be modified to take in one or more of four wineries that lie within easy reach (see Map 22). The closest is Pilliterri Winery, which lies just to the northeast of Virgil. Reif, Inniskillin, and Marynissen wineries lie slightly to the south of the tour.

Map 22, Niagara-on-the-Lake bicycle tour

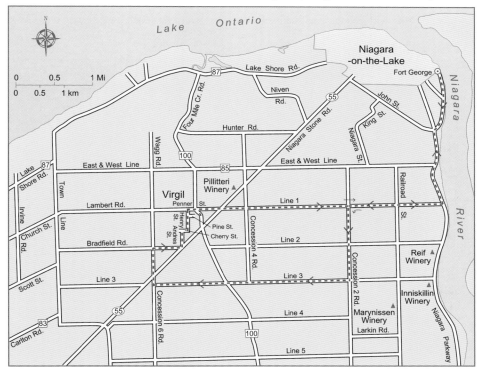

The bicycle is the most efficient means yet invented for converting human energy into propulsion. The first self-propelled bicycle was invented in 1839 by Kirkpatrick Macmillan, a blacksmith in Scotland. However, his model, which was relatively heavy with its iron-rimmed wheels, never became popular. In 1861, Pierre Michaux and his son built a bicycle in Paris that immediately caught on, although it was known as the "boneshaker" because of its rigid wood and iron frame. The first recorded bicycle race was held on May 31, 1868 from Paris to Rouen.

TOUR 2:
West of St. Catharines *(Map 23)*

This 30 kilometre (19 mile) tour visits orchards and vineyards as well as two wineries. There are some ups and downs to be negotiated at the south end of the loop as the road climbs the Niagara Escarpment. We suggest you start the tour at the Rockway community centre on Pelham Road (Regional Road 69) and proceed clockwise as shown on Map 23.

Go west along Pelham Road and turn right at 9th Street. The Rockway Glen golf course is on the left at about the 2.5 kilometre (1.5 mile) mark and refreshments are available at the club house.

An optional extra at about the 12 kilometre (7.4 mile) mark is to continue west along the North Service Road of the QEW Highway instead of turning right onto Gregory Road. After about one kilometre, you will reach the gates to Charles Daly Park, a pleasant lakeside park with swimming and picnic grounds.

At about 14.7 kilometres (9.1 miles), shortly after you have turned right onto 3rd Avenue, you will see

Cycling in Niagara

CLAUDETTE LOSIER

the Green Ribbon Trail on the left. This is a pleasant side trip and takes you down to a pond covered in water-lily pads and then to the memorial for missing children.

At about the 25.1 kilometre (15.6 mile) point, as you cycle westward along Eighth Avenue, instead of turning left on Fifth Street, make a small detour by heading straight ahead on Eighth Avenue to Hernder Estates winery. This pretty winery is set in a 130-year-old Victorian barn, and you cycle through Niagara's only covered bridge to enter the property.

Return along Eighth Avenue and turn right (south) on Fifth Street. Henry of Pelham winery awaits you at the next corner. Wine tastings are offered at both wineries.

Perhaps weaving slightly, you now have some hill work left to complete the southern end of the tour and return to the Rockway Community Centre.

TOUR 3:
Pelham and the Short Hills
(Map 23)

This tour, contributed by Fran Bauer, mother of the legendary Canadian cyclist Steve Bauer, is one of the prettiest in the Niagara area – but you have to work as there are many hills. We suggest you start this 33-kilometre (20 mile) ride at Rockway Community Centre on Pelham Road (Regional Road 69) west of St. Catharines and follow Map 23 in a counter-clockwise direction.

Go west along Pelham Road for a short distance and then turn left onto

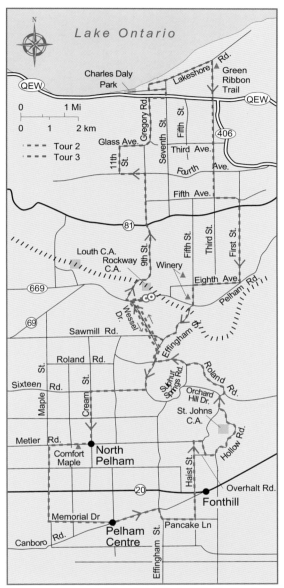

Map 23, West of St. Catharines;
Pelham and the Short Hills

Wessel Drive. The route is easy to follow. At about the 8 kilometre (5 mile) mark, just past the right turn onto Metler Road, a sign will

Comfort Maple in Fall

announce the Comfort Maple. This very short detour is well worth the time, as the Comfort Maple, at about 500 years, is the oldest sugar Maple tree in Canada. And quite a sight it is too, with its gnarled trunk and branches supported by guy wires reaching as high as a ten-storey building (34 metres or 112 feet). Old Glory, as it is called by the Comfort family who farm the surrounding land, towers majestically over neighbouring orchards.

Another jewel along this tour is Edward's, a large gracious century home at about kilometre 15 (mile 9.3) on the right side at 398 Canboro Road. This red brick house with ornate trim and its accompanying old barn is a reminder of prosperous country living in bygone days.

A good place to stop for a rest is at about the two-thirds mark at the intersection of Haist Street and Highway 20. The Loft Restaurant and Ice Cream Parlour is on the north side of Highway 20 just a little west of the corner. This is a favourite place for the Freewheelers to stop and partake of sustenance before tackling the winding, rolling lanes of Short Hills that lead back to the Rockway Community Centre.

TOUR 4:
South of Niagara (Map 24)

This flat ride of about 45 kilometres (28 miles) travels the Niagara Parkway and then winds its way through the farm lands above the escarpment. This area has quite a different character from the farm lands below the escarpment, with mostly dairy farming and crops such as corn.

The parking lot at Kingsbridge Park, Chippawa, is suggested as a starting point. The first part of the tour winds along the Niagara River. The rest of the route, as shown on Map 24, is quite easy to follow.

A stop at Nigh's Sweet Shop at the Snydor intersection is highly recommended as their chocolates are famous across the peninsula.

A good place to replenish your energy reserves is at Dora's Place restaurant on the east side of Sodom Road, just north of Sherk Road.

TOUR 5:
The Ferry-Ride Tour (Map 24)
Although relatively long at 73 kilometres (45 miles), this is a rewarding tour as it offers a thorough overview of Niagara including the Niagara Parkway, farmlands above and below the escarpment, as well as a section along the Welland Canal.

The Port Robinson Ferry
On August 24, 1974, the downbound ship Steelton, crashed into the vertical-lift bridge at Port Robinson before it was fully raised. The village, which straddles the canal, was effectively cut in half. Rather than building a new bridge, a passenger ferry was installed that has operated ever since. The Town of Thorold is responsible for managing the ferry.

The highlight of the tour is a (free) crossing of the Welland Canal on Niagara's only ferry.

The suggested starting point is at Queenston Heights Park, where there is ample parking. Follow the tour in a clockwise direction as shown on Map

The Edward House

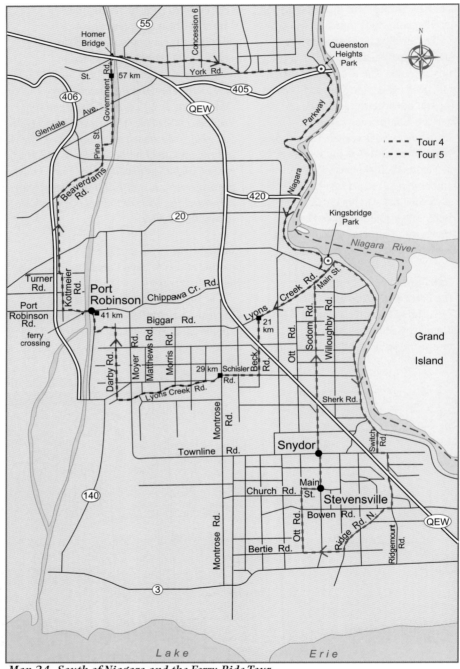

Map 24, South of Niagara and the Ferry-Ride Tour

24. Proceed along the Niagara Recreational Trail until Chippawa. Cross the bridge and turn right onto Main Street, which becomes Lyons Creek Road.

Note that at about 21 kilometres (13 miles), the left turn onto Beck Road is easy to miss, as is the left turn (actually a fork) onto Lyons Creek Road at about kilometre 29 (mile 18). Ignore the No Exit sign at the corner of Morris Road and Lyons Creek Road and proceed; you can carry your bike across the railway tracks. At the next intersection (Matthews Road) is a historical marker commemorating the Battle of Cook's Mills, which took place here in 1814.

When you reach the Welland Canal along Biggar Road, take a moment to see how the Welland River is diverted under the Welland Canal by the use of siphons, so that their waters do not mix.

When you reach Port Robinson, turn left on Bridge Street for the ferry. If you are with a large group note that the ferry only has a capacity of six people (it does not take cars and does not operate during the mid-winter months i.e. when the Canal is frozen). The Knockerheads Tavern at kilometre 41 (mile 25.4) is a good place for a rest while you await the ferry.

To get through Thorold:
➤ turn left off Beaverdams Road onto Pine Street
➤ turn right onto Richmond Street (at traffic lights)
➤ turn right onto Lynden Street (at beer store)
➤ jog right, then left onto Government Road which is beside the Canal and follow it north.

The Lock 3 Museum Complex at kilometre 57 (mile 35.3) is an excellent place for a rest, nourishment, and to watch giant ships move through the lock. The steel deck on the Homer Bridge crossing at kilometre 58 (mile 36) is treacherous. We strongly recommend that you walk your bike across.

An alternate, and pleasant, ending to this route is to proceed along Queenston Road until Concession 6 at which point you turn right, followed by a left on York Road. Soon you will see the magnificent edifice of Château des Charmes winery with its beckoning tasting rooms.

At kilometre 71 (mile 44) take the bike pathway, which is about 300 metres before the intersection of York Road and the Niagara Parkway, for the final climb up the escarpment. We hope your tired legs make it.

TOUR 6:
The Grand Tour of Niagara

For those who would like to gain a very thorough overview of the Niagara area in one tour, we recommend this ambitious Grand Tour of Niagara. This circle tour goes the entire length of both the beautiful Niagara Parkway and the Welland Canal as well as the joining sections along lakes Erie and Ontario. The tour offers a rich look at Niagara and includes the mighty Niagara Falls, the historic forts at Fort Erie and Niagara-on-the-Lake, several wineries, the engineering feat and massive ships of the Welland Canal, lush orchards and vineyards, numerous picnic spots, and much more.

Although some intrepid cyclists will take this tour by bicycle, most people will prefer to do it by car. There is so much to see that you may wish to allow two or more days and spend the night(s) at some of the charming bed and breakfast establishments along the way.

We will describe the tour in a counter-clockwise direction, assuming a starting point at the Lock 3 viewing complex. Start by following the Welland Canal south as described in Tours 3 and 4 in Chapter 7. On reaching Port Colborne consider making a visit to the Port Colborne Historical and Marine Museum at 280 King Street (King runs parallel to and one west of the Canal). Proceed south to Clarence Street, turn left, and cross the (southernmost) bridge.

Proceed due east along Durham Road (be careful to get off the main street as it curves to the left soon after crossing the bridge). In about a mile, the road turns south and becomes Reuter Road. Soon it curves left and follows the lakeshore heading east. This section is short but pleasant with many gracious summer cottages along the lakefront.

At Lorraine Road, you turn north and then east at Highway 3. After about five kilometres (three miles), veer southeast onto Sherkston Road. Proceed until Sherkston merges with Michener Road and follow it east to Ridge Road. Make a right turn (to the south) and immediately turn to the east. Follow Thunder Bay Road, a very small track that services the

lakeside cottages, toward Fort Erie. At Stonemill Road, there is a small left and right jog onto MacDonald Drive. MacDonald Drive wends its way up to Dominion Road, a major artery. Turn right and follow it to historic Fort Erie (see Chapter 5), which is an excellent place to stop and rest.

Proceed in an easterly direction, keeping as close to the river as possible. You will pass the Peace Bridge, a commercial area, and finally you will join the Niagara Parkway. The many attractions of the world-famous Niagara Parkway are described in Chapters 4 and 5.

Follow the Niagara Parkway north until you reach the Town of Niagara-on-the-Lake (see Chapter 12).

At Niagara-on-the-Lake, follow Mary Street west until it becomes Lakeshore Road. Follow this all the way to the Welland Canal, passing through some of the most bountiful orchards in Canada (see Map 22). Tasty stops can be made at the many road-side fruit stands.

Cross the Welland Canal at Lock 1 and turn immediately south and proceed along the west bank of the canal back to Lock 3. Congratulations on completing one of the most scenic and rewarding tours in Canada!

The entire journey is about 145 kilometres (90 miles) long comprised of the following segments (distances are approximate).

Welland Canal:	40 km (25 miles)
Lake Erie:	35 km (22 miles)
Niagara Parkway:	55 km (34 miles)
Lake Ontario:	15 km (9 miles)

Chapter 15

FOR ROCK HOUNDS

For those who are fascinated by the scientific intricacies of palaeontology, sedimentology, glaciology, and crystallography, or for those who are simply avid rock hounds, we recommend the following places to find pet rocks.

Tour 1:
The Niagara Glen

There are many places in the Niagara area that offer excellent exposures of strata of the Silurian and Ordovician periods. One of the best is at Niagara Glen (see Chapter 5 for location and more details), where the gorge cut by the Niagara River has laid bare rocks dating to over 450 million years ago. The Glen is also a very pleasant place to picnic, where the (non-rock-struck) family members can pleasantly while away the time while you immerse yourself in more earthy things.

A word of caution: The Niagara Glen is a nature preserve and collecting fossils is not permitted.

As you leave the parking lot heading toward the gorge, a descent of about 2 metres marks the bank of what was the Niagara River about 9,000 years ago. The flat picnic area, Wilson Terrace, was the old river bed, and the water flowed along it forming a falls as it dropped over the cliff at the northern end. In those ancient days, an island separated this channel from another one along the US side, which had its own falls. The island, undercut by the river, collapsed long ago, and its remnants form the northern tip of Wilson Terrace.

The geologic formations at the Glen are exposed over several flats and terraces as shown in the figure, ranging from the Queenston dolostone (also known as the Lockport limestone) at the top, to the Queenston shale (also known as the Red Medina shale) at the bottom of the gorge, with limestones, shales, and sandstones in between. These rocks represent about 40 million years of geologic evolution from the upper Ordovician (about 460 million years ago) to the middle Silurian (about 420 million years ago).

Eurypterids
Commonly called sea scorpions, Eurypterids are distantly related to the modern horseshoe crab. It had a flounder-like body with 12 moveable segments on its back and a sharp, dagger-like tail. Depending on the species, it had from one to four pairs of legs.

Potholes, bowl-shaped or cylindrical hollows, form in limestone rocks when the energy of cascading water causes a stone along with gravel and sand to swirl in a depression. Acting over decades and centuries, potholes several metres in size can be ground out of solid rock. Some excellent examples of potholes are found in the Glen.

Geology at Niagara Glen

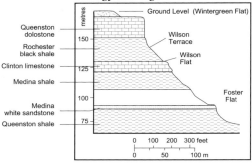

Fossils are also found here, including trilobites (elliptical shaped crustaceans), eurypterids (commonly known as sea scorpions), crinoids (sea lilies), and corals. Complete fossils are rare as wave action and the weight of overlying deposits has left mostly fragments preserved in the rocks. A coral reef is located under the overhang of the Queenston dolostone, north of the metal staircase.

Niagara area fossils

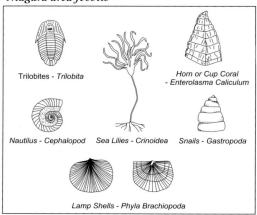

Tour 2:
The Museum

The Schoellkopf Geological Museum in Niagara Falls, New York (see Chapter 4, Tour 3 for location and details) is devoted almost entirely to the geology of Niagara Falls with explanations of the 435 million-year history of the gorge and the 12,000 years of the Falls recession. It contains excellent exhibits, and tours of the gorge are offered by State Park geologists and naturalists.

Tour 3:
The Quarry

Some wonderful fossils can be found at an abandoned limestone quarry west of Port Colborne, Ontario. Take highway 58 south and turn west on Highway 3 to Quarrie Road. Turn south and proceed about a mile. Park at the side of the road near the bridge.

Owned by the Niagara Peninsula Conservation Authority, this site is one of the most popular fossil collecting sites in the province. The quarry contains fossils created in the middle Devonian period some 380 million years ago in a tropical sea that covered the region. The rocks consist of limestone of the Onandaga Formation with a large array of corral fossilization including solitary and tabulate corals. Crinoid stems, brachiopods, and trilobites can also be found.

A word of caution. This spot is popular with teenagers who come to swim in the flooded quarry on hot days. You may wish to avoid this quarry on summer weekends if you

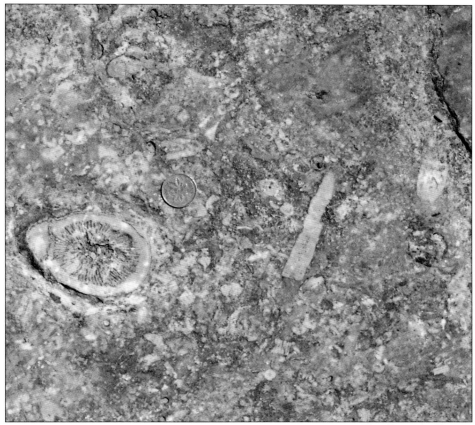

Fossils at the Quarry

are offended by loud music, swearing, and immature behaviour.

Tour 4:
Quaternary Geology

Those interested in soft rocks, that is the soils that lie above the bedrock, should explore near Beacon Harbourside Inn and at Charles Daly Park, both of which are located on Lake Ontario, east of Jordan Harbour, Ontario. There you will find some good exposures of lacustrine (lake) deposits, which were laid down by the ancient Lake Iroquois, from about 12,500 years ago. These deposits are underlain by an older glacial till.

Regional Road 81 (also known as Highway 8) follows approximately along the old shoreline of Lake Iroquois. As you drive along this road west of St. Catharines, perhaps while on a tour of the wineries, looking north you will see gently sloping, flat lands that formed in Lake Iroquois. This is excellent fruit growing country with cherries and peaches predominating nearer the lake on well drained sandy soils and apples, pears, and grapes dominating on the land nearer the highway where the soil contains more clay.

On the south side of the road, the land rising up to the escarpment is more irregular, showing that the soils were deposited by the action of glaciers.

Other Geologic Points of Interest

A good spot to observe palaeozoic strata, similar to that in the Niagara Gorge, is along the road cut made for Burleigh Hill Drive, where it climbs the escarpment in St. Catharines. Burleigh Hill Drive is elongated approximately north-south between Glendale Avenue at the north and St. Davids Road at the south, parallel to and east of Highway 406. Park your car on one of the side streets at either the top or bottom of the escarpment. The road cut reveals excellent exposures of the base of the Queenston dolostone underlain by the Rochester shale. If you have sharp eyes you will find fossils such as crinoids, trilobites, and brachiopods.

Queenston Quarry: Started by a Scottish stonemason, this quarry has operated continuously for over 160 years and is one of the oldest in Canada. The Queenston dolostone (also known as the Lockport limestone) is quarried and has been used in building the locks of the second Welland Canal, Brock's monument, Oak Hall, Canada House in London, England, and the Hamilton post office, to name a few. Entrance to this quarry can only be obtained by special permission from Redland Quarries Inc.-Queenston, although some of the non-working areas can be viewed in the Queenston Trails walk (see Tour 1, Chapter 9).

Natural gas was originally found near Dufferin Islands in about 1794 and has provided many farmers and others living above the escarpment a source of heating fuel since that time. The gas emanates from the Red Medina shale and has been trapped by the overlying impervious Clinton shale and limestone. Today there are still hundreds of private gas wells in operation.

Three caves are found north of Hubbard Point on the Canadian side of the Niagara Gorge, a few hundred metres downstream from the Rainbow Bridge. Created when the falls were at this place, the caves are irregular in shape with depths of approximately ten metres (33 feet). They contain some features of interest such as stalactites. Unfortunately, they can not be visited without climbing equipment and permission from the Niagara Parks Commission.

More Information

Further information about the geology of the Niagara area, including the formation of Niagara Falls, the geology of wine growing, and much more, can be obtained by contacting the Department of Earth Sciences at Brock University, St. Catharines at (905) 688-5550, extension 3526. An excellent summary of local geology is presented by A.H. Tiplin (see Bibliography).

Chapter 16

THE SEASONS

Magnolia blossoms

Although most people will tour the Niagara area in summer, the other seasons are also very special. This chapter explores the magic of these non peak-time seasons and provides tips on where their special qualities can best be observed.

Spring

Maple syrup. About the middle of March, when the land is still in the icy grip of winter, there is a sign that warmer days are just around the corner. The maple trees, through some ancient skill, recognize that Old Man Winter is weakening his grip and a sugary sap begins to course in their veins. Each spring, the Niagara Peninsula Conservation Authority taps this rich syrup and holds demonstrations and tastings at the Vineland Quarries Sugarbush. There is no better way to thumb your nose at Old Man Winter than to partake in this tasty operation. For details see Maple Syrup Days in Chapter 17.

Spring is a time of rebirth. Trees that only a few short weeks ago were naked and scrawny now don delicate wraps of pink and white blossoms. Niagara, with its multitude of orchards, is a wonderful area for viewing blossoms in the spring. During a brief period, usually in the second and third weeks of May, every backroad is transformed into a magical showcase. The trees are dressed up for a formal coming out ball before getting on with their work of producing fruit. Trees wearing dazzling white debutante dresses are lined up in neatly tended fields where the smell of freshly-ploughed soil mingles with the sweet fragrance of blossoms.

Trilliums. One of the best spots to view thousands of trilliums carpeting the forest floor, dappled by sunlight filtering through the forest canopy, is at St. Johns Conservation Area (see Chapter 10, Tour 2).

Another great spring wildflower spot is the Louth Conservation Area (Chapter 9, Tour 4), where the forest floor is covered with delicate white trilliums as well as Dutchman's britches and trout lilies.

Blossoms, blossoms, blossoms. We recommend drives along the back roads below the escarpment, such as around Virgil or along Lakeshore Road. A place we like to go is Queenston Heights park (Chapter 5), where cherry blossoms are a brilliant pink in the sunshine. Another special place that we visit every spring is the Niagara Parks Commission Greenhouse (Chapter 4, Tour 2), in front of which is a splendid row of magnolias that have the most beautiful white and pink blossoms of any trees in the area.

Making maple syrup at the Sugar Bush

NIAGARA PENINSULA CONSERVATION AUTHORITY

Dufferin Islands with fall colours

Fall

As summer turns into fall, the nights become cooler and the days, although rapidly becoming shorter, are blessed with dry, sunny weather. The days are still sunny and warm, but the humidity dissipates and the trees are ablaze with colour. The fall is a wonderful time to enjoy walks and tours in the Niagara area.

One of the best places to observe the leaves in their annual riot of colour is along the Niagara Parkway from Queenston Heights to Niagara-on-the-Lake. This section of the Parkway has some majestic old trees

Pumpkin field in the fall

that are splendid at any time of year but are in their full glory in the fall.

Dufferin Islands (Chapter 4, Tour 2) is a favourite spot for photographers in the fall when the calm pools reflect the brilliant foliage.

The Bruce Trail is also at its best in the fall, and we recommend visits to DeCew Falls and Balls Falls to see the waterfalls contrasted against the colourful canopy of the Carolinian forest.

The fall also brings the harvesting of the grape and the joy of wine making. There are many special events associated with the wineries in the fall, and this is a particularly good time to tour the many boutique wineries (see Chapter 11) and enjoy not only the excellent vintages but also the multi-coloured countryside.

Winter

In Niagara, winter is a time of contrasts. It is a season of Dr. Jekyll and Mr. Hyde. One day the earth is covered with a pristine blanket of virgin snow, everything exuding a serene innocence and elegance. But the next day, mild weather brings melting and slush. Now everything is drab in the winter monotone of dreary brown.

Yet many of our best memories of Niagara are from the winter season. And there is no better place to experience winter than at Niagara Falls itself, which is set like a jewel in frozen splendour. The constant mist rising from the roaring cascades coats and freezes on every tree twig, every lamp post, every railing, creating a sparkling surreal wonderland – it is like a magical kingdom where everything is made of crystal. It is a

The Falls transform to a crystal wonderland in winter

Ice and sun

photographer's delight with sunlight dancing, shimmering, and bending in wonderful prismatic effects from the ice coatings. And the effect is greatly enhanced by the backdrop of the mighty Falls and its thunder.

There is another wonderful sight to behold at the Falls, although it does not occur every year. Warm spells accompanied by strong west-

Wintery road at Burgoyne Woods, St. Catharines, Ontario

erly or southwesterly winds can break up the ice that has formed along the shores of Lake Erie and send huge ice floes racing down the Niagara River. The ice floes are broken into smaller pieces by the rapids and tumble over the Falls. When the ice reaches the eddy

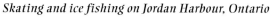

Skating and ice fishing on Jordan Harbour, Ontario

Sunday crowd on the ice bridge, circa 1893

current near the Maid of the Mist docks, it is forced toward the Canadian shore where it jams. As the river brings more and more ice, the mass grows like a giant log jam with the crevassed appearance of a glacier. Once the winds subside, the water level drops leaving the ice mass suspended like a bridge.

In the late 1800s, the ice bridges became a popular tourist attraction and huts selling everything from souvenirs to coffee to hard liquor were set up on the ice. The public's fascination and enjoyment of this spectacle lasted until 1912, when three people were swept to their deaths when the ice bridge broke up without warning. Since that time, crossing the river on the ice bridge has been prohibited. In 1938, during a thaw, combined with an 80 kilometre per hour (50 mile per hour) southwest wind, the river filled with ice from Niagara-on-the-Lake to the Horseshoe Falls to such an enormous extent that it toppled the Upper Steel Arch Bridge.

Since 1964, an ice boom constructed of logs has been installed across the mouth of the river each winter. Ice bridges still form part of the Niagara winter scene, but they are not as immense and spectacular as in the days before the boom.

Winter also forms the stage for the Festival of Lights, which usually runs from late November to mid January and features colourful lighting displays as well as entertainment at an outdoor stage near the Falls. Combined with the nightly illumination of the Falls, it transforms the area into a spectacular palette of colour.

Some of our favorite winter walks are along the Bruce Trail. The countryside is silent and you can walk in complete solitude. Waterfalls such as DeCew and Ball's Falls are frozen into delicate chandeliers of ice.

The cross-country skiing aficionado can strap on the boards and glide through the snow at Whirlpool golf course, Short Hills Provincial Park, and Woodend Conservation Area.

Chapter 17

FESTIVALS, FAIRS AND SPECIAL EVENTS

Niagara Falls Festival of Lights

There are many festivals and other special events that not only capture the special character and atmosphere of Niagara but are also a lot of fun. They are listed below in chronological order with brief descriptions. For more detailed information, call or write the Chamber of Commerce or Tourist Bureau for the city or town in which the event is being held. The numbers and addresses are listed in the Appendix.

Ongoing Events

Artpark: April until October. Musical theatre, jazz festival, art workshops, National ballet of Canada, pop and jazz concerts, 200-acre park located in Lewiston, NY. 1-800-659-7275

Shaw Festival: April through October. Plays by George Bernard Shaw and his contemporary playwrights presented in three locations in Niagara-on-the-Lake, Ontario. 1-800-511-SHAW

Fireworks over Niagara Falls:
every Friday from mid-May until the end of August.
Can be viewed (free) from either side of the border at 10 pm.
Also presented on Victoria Day (May), Memorial Day (May), Canada Day (July 1), and Independence Day (July 4).

Old Fort Niagara:
throughout the year.
Military re-enactment, battles, grand reviews, historic tent camps, fife and drums. Youngstown, NY.
Call (716) 745-7611 for details.

Winter Festival of Lights:
end of November until early January.
Featuring Disney's famous light displays. Both sides of the border.

March
Maple Syrup Days:
usually last three weekends of March.
Demonstrations of historical and modern methods of making maple syrup. A demonstration trail and guided tours. The Vineland Quarries Sugar Bush is operated by the Niagara Peninsula Conservation Authority. The Sugar Bush is on the east side of Cherry Avenue between Moyer and Fly Roads, Vineland, Ontario.
(905) 680-PARK

May
The Virgil Stampede: mid-May.
Rodeo competitions, midway, craft show, fireworks.
At the Virgil Fairgrounds, Virgil, Ont.

June
Port Dalhousie Alive: mid-June.
Live music, street performers, buskers, family entertainment, 5 cent rides on the 100-year-old restored carousel in the park. Port Dalhousie is the lake-side suburb of St. Catharines, Ontario.

Tour De Vin:
last two weekends in June.
Receive a passport and get it stamped as you tour the Niagara-on-the-Lake, Ontario wineries with special winemakers selections available at each stop. Tour by car or by bicycle.
(905) 468-3554

Loch Sloy Highland Games: late June.
Scottish dancers, food and music, heavy games, massed pipe bands.
Free admission - Historic Fort Erie, Ontario.

Welland Rose Festival:
usually middle two weeks of June.
Annual Horticultural Society Rose Show, sporting tournaments, arts & crafts, and the Rose Parade.
Welland, Ontario.
(905) 732-6603

July
Canada Day celebrations at Niagara-on-the-Lake: on July 1.
Simcoe Park: games, contests and activities for children, music for adults. Fort George: period demonstrations, evening of music, artillery demonstrations, and spectacular fireworks. Niagara-on-the-Lake, Ont.

Fort Erie battle re-enactment

<u>Fort Erie-Buffalo Friendship Festival:</u>
July 1-4. Concerts, air show, crafts
show, midway, Canada Day and Independence Day fireworks.
Free admission - entrance at Mather
Arch, Fort Erie, Ontario.
(905) 871-8525

<u>Vineyard Jazz:</u> mid-July.
Held at the Hillebrand Estates
winery, Virgil, Ontario, featuring
international and local jazz musi-
cians. Food and wine available.
(905) 468-7123

<u>A Taste of Buffalo:</u> mid-July.
Restaurants across the city come
together for a marvellous food
spectacular. Main St., Buffalo, NY.
(716) 831-9376

<u>War of 1812 Re-enactment:</u>
end of July.
Fort George in Niagara-on-the-Lake,
Ontario, becomes the target of
artillery bombardment and
invading forces. Relive the War of
1812 as British and American
infantry stage mock battles amongst
the period encampments.
(905) 468-4257

<u>Four Weekends in July:</u>
Four special weekends in which all
Niagara wineries participate with
wine tastings and specially guided
tours of the wine cellars, BBQs on the
bistro decks, jazz concerts, and more.
Bicycle or drive along the Niagara
Wine Route.
1-800-ONTARIO

Prince of Wales Stakes:
late July or early August.
This thoroughbred horse race is the
second jewel in Canada's Triple
Crown. Held at Fort Erie, Ontario
Racetrack.

August
Royal Henley Regatta:
first two weeks of August.
World class rowing on the Henley
course on Martindale Pond,
St. Catharines, Ontario.
(905) 684-2361

Canal Days: first weekend of August.
Celebrating the marine heritage of
Port Colborne and the Welland Canal.
At the Port Colborne Museum, 280
King Street, Port Colborne, Ontario.
(905) 834-7604

Peach of a Weekend: mid August.
Celebrate the peach harvest with
entertainment, a parade, and peach
delights prepared by Niagara's top
chefs. Niagara-on-the-Lake, Ontario.
(905) 468-4263

Tastes of Niagara: late August.
Brings together Niagara, Ontario,
food producers, restaurateurs, chefs,
and vintners to provide gourmet local
cuisine. Call Vision Niagara,
(905) 646-3362

September
Niagara Regional Exhibition:
second week of September.
Showplace for Niagara agriculture
since 1857. Featuring farm animals,
exhibits, midway and special attractions. Welland, Ontario.

Niagara Grape and Wine Festival:
last two weeks of September.
Many different events, winery tours
and tastings, gourmet dinners, 10
km road race, Grand Parade, Event in
the Tent with live bands, family
entertainment.
St. Catharines, Ontario.
(905) 688-0212

Jazz and Dixieland Festival:
late September.
Amherst, New York.
(716) 634-1863

October
Niagara Food Festival:
first weekend in October.
Niagara chefs present their best
dishes and wineries offer their vintages, live music and cooking demonstrations. Held on Merritt Island,
Welland, Ontario.

Thanksgiving Festival Craft Show &
Sale: Thanksgiving Weekend.
Ball's Falls Conservation Area, near
Vineland, Ontario.
Crafts, demonstrations, food in the
restored pioneer village.

Inside mill at Ball's Falls

Jordan Pioneer Days: Mid-October.
Jordan Historical Museum - 3802
Main St., Jordan, Ontario.
Enjoy a trip back in time with period
and military dress and demonstrations of pioneering skills and crafts.
(905) 684-5478

North America's largest family-
oriented New Year's Eve celebrations:
Non-alcoholic celebrations and live
entertainment in conjunction with
the Festival of Lights, Victoria Park,
Niagara Falls, Ontario.

December
Candlelight Stroll through Niagara-
on-the-Lake, Ontario:
first weekend of December.
Join the stroll winding through the
historical town, with Christmas
entertainment and carols by local
choirs.

Chapter 18

BIBLIOGRAPHY

Andrist, Ralph, K., **The Erie Canal**, American Heritage Publishing Co. Inc., New York, 1964.

Berton, P., **Niagara – A History of the Falls**, McClelland & Stewart Inc., Toronto, 1992.

Borrello, Joe, **Wineries of the Great Lakes: A Guidebook**, Raptor Press, Lapeer, MI, 1995.

Bramble, Linda, **Undiscovered Niagara**, The Boston Mills Press, Erin, Ontario, 1990.

Field, J.L., **Niagara-on-the-Lake Guidebook**, Copyright J.L. Field, Niagara-on-the-Lake, 1984.

Hilts, S., and P. Mitchell, **Caring for Your Land: A Stewardship Handbook for Niagara Escarpment Landowners**, Centre for Land and Water Stewardship, University of Guelph, 1994.

Jackson, J.N., **The Four Welland Canals – A Journey of Discovery in St. Catharines and Thorold**, Vanwell Publishing Limited, St. Catharines, Ontario, 1988.

Jackson, J.N. and S.M. Wilson, **St. Catharines – Canada's Canal City**, St. Catharines Standard Limited, St. Catharines, Ontario, 1992.

Keough, P. and R., **The Niagara Escarpment – A Portfolio**, Stoddart Publishing Co. Limited, Don Mills, Ontario, 1990.

Kiwanis Club of Stamford, Ontario, Inc., **Niagara – River of Fame**, Ainsworth Press Inc., Kitchener, Ontario, 1986.

Lamb, L. and G. Rhynard, **Plants of Carolinian Canada**, Federation of Ontario Naturalists, Don Mills, Ontario, 1994.

Mason, Philip D., **Niagara – A guide to the Niagara Frontier with maps and photographs**, Travelpic Publications, Niagara Falls, Ontario, 1965.

Rannie, William, F., **Cave Springs Farm: In Lore and Legend**, W.F.Rannie - Publisher, Lincoln, Ontario.

Seibel, George A., **Ontario's Niagara Parks – A History**, Niagara Parks Commission, 1985.

Stokes, P.J., **Old Niagara on the Lake**, University of Toronto Press, Toronto, 1971.

Tiplin, Albert H., **Our Romantic Niagara – A Geological History of the River and the Falls**, The Niagara Falls Heritage Foundation, Niagara Falls, Ontario, 1988.

$\mathcal{A}$ppendix

HELPFUL ORGANIZATIONS

Further information on the tours and points of interest can be obtained from the following sources (all telephone numbers are in area code 905, unless shown otherwise):

Brocks Monument
Queenston Heights Park
262-4759
Park and picnic areas, the start of the Bruce trail, monument to General
Sir Isaac Brock.

Bruce Trail Association (Niagara Chapter)
Box 22042
St. Catharines, Ontario L2T 4C1
Hikes of varying lengths and degrees of difficulty are regularly scheduled.
Or call Bruce Trail Association office in Hamilton at 800 665-HIKE

(Greater) Buffalo Convention and Visitors Bureau
107 Delaware Avenue
Buffalo, NY 14202
(716) 852-0511 or 1-800-BUFFALO
Internet: http:\\www.moran.com/buffalo

Destination Niagara on the Internet
http://www.tourismniagara.com

Dufferin Islands Nature Area
356-2241
Nature area, walking trails, a children's swimming area, and viewing point
for the upper rapids.

Economic Development Corporation of Fort Erie
121 Garrison Rd., Fort Erie, Ontario L2A 6G6
871-1332 or 871-8525
Internet: http://tourismniagara.com/forterie

Fort Erie Chamber of Commerce
427 Garrison Rd., Fort Erie, Ontario
871-3803

Fort George, Niagara-on-the-Lake
468-4257
Built by the British in 1797, open for touring May - October

Historic Fort Erie
871-0540
Fort used in the War of 1812. Museum and military displays
daily in the summer.

New York Power Authority
Niagara Power Authority, Community Relations Division
P.O. Box 277
Niagara Falls, NY 14302
(716) 285-3211

Niagara County Tourism
139 Niagara Street
Lockport, New York 14094
1-800 338-7890

Niagara Economic and Tourism Corporation (NET Corp.)
P.O. Box 1042, Thorold, Ontario L2V 4T7
984-3626 or 1-800-263-2988
Internet: http://www.tourismniagara.com

Niagara Falls Chamber of Commerce
4394 Queen St., Niagara Falls, Ontario
374-3666

Niagara Falls, NY Convention and Visitors Bureau
310 4th Street
Niagara Falls, NY 14303
(716) 285-2400
Internet: http:\\nfvcb.com

Niagara Falls, Ontario Visitor and Convention Bureau
5433 Victoria Ave.
Niagara Falls, Ontario L2G 3L1
(905) 356-6061   FX (905) 356-5567
Internet: http:\\tourismniagara.com/NFCVCB

Niagara Freewheelers Bicycle Touring Club Inc.
Box 23118
Midtown Post Office
124 Welland Avenue
St. Catharines, Ontario L2R 7P6

Niagara Nature Tours
Box 25, Jordan Station, Ontario L0R 1S0
562-4154
Year round tours by qualified naturalists, for all ages, and some
are wheelchair accessible. All tours are rated for difficulty.

Niagara-on-the-Lake Chamber of Commerce
153 King St, Niagara-on-the-Lake, Ontario L0S 1J0
468-4263

Niagara Parks Commission
Offices at Oak Hall, across from Marineland in Niagara Falls, Ontario.
Box 150, Niagara Falls, Ontario L2E 6T2
356-7944 (Mid-May to mid-October)
356-2241 (all other times)
NPC will provide a visitors guide, recreational trail brochure,
information on Battlefields associated with the War of 1812,
the Niagara Glen, Horticulture School, Queenston Heights and Brock's
Monument, Spanish Aero Car, Great Gorge Adventure, Journey
Behind the Falls.

Niagara Glen Nature Reserve
On the Niagara River Parkway, north of Niagara Falls, Ontario.
Free guided nature walks late June until Labour Day.

Niagara Peninsula Conservation Authority
2358 Centre Street, Allanburg, Ontario L0S 1A0
680-PARK (7275) or 1-800-263-4760
NPCA has 34 conservation areas in the region providing
opportunities for swimming, camping, hiking, canoeing,
picnicking and nature studies. Further information, maps
and descriptions can be obtained by contacting the NPCA.

Old Fort Niagara
Youngstown, New York
(716) 745-7611
Original 18th century French/British fortress. Demonstrations daily in summer. Open daily year round.

Parks and Recreation Departments
St. Catharines	688-5601
Niagara Falls	356-7521
Niagara-on-the-Lake	468-4261
Welland	732-7300
Fort Erie	871-1600
Port Colborne	835-2900

Parks and Recreation Departments have lists of parks, public swimming pools, hiking trails within their area.

Port Colborne Chamber of Commerce
76 Main St. West, Port Colborne, Ontario
834-9765

Port Colborne Economic and Tourism Development Department
239 King St., Port Colborne, Ontario L3K 4G8
1-888-PORT FUN
Internet: www.portcolborne.com

St. Catharines Chamber of Commerce
11 King St., St. Catharines, Ontario L2R 6Z4
684-2361 FX 684-2100

Scout Shop
32 Cherry Street, St. Catharines, Ontario L2R 5M6
905 685-8600
Orienteering maps of Short Hills.

Thorold Chamber of Commerce
3 Front Street North
Thorold, Ontario L2V 1X3
680-4233

Welland Canal Lock Three Complex
685-3711
Raised viewing platform, museum, picnic sites, directly on the Welland Canal recreation Trail.

Welland Chamber of Commerce
32 East Main St., Welland, Ontario
732-7515

Wine Council of Ontario
110 Hanover Drive, Suite B205
St. Catharines, Ontario L2W 1A4
684-8070 FX 684-2993
The Wine Council will provide a calender of events including
winemakers tastings, specially guided tours, and special events
such as BBQs, jazz concerts, and bike tours.

Index

Acknowledgements

Many people have provided the encouragement, support, and ideas to help bring this endeavour to fruition. We would like to thank the following: Margaret Dunn, who led the way by self-publishing her own book and providing us with many pointers; Rose Ellen Campbell, Campbell Creative Services, whose artistic hand designed the layout for this book; Tom Torrance for carefully editing the manuscript; Eveline Stout, Paul Pattison and other members of the Niagara Freewheelers Bicycle Touring Club; Brenda Zadoroznij, Niagara Bruce Trail Club; Ron Dale, Canadian Heritage, Parks Canada; Roberta Veley and members of the Steering Committee for the Niagara Gateway Project; Gary Hardy, Niagara Economic and Tourism Corporation; Len Pennachetti, Vintners Quality Alliance; Ray Cadorette, Niagara Credit Union; William Rickers, St. Catharines Chamber of Commerce; Evelyn Janke, Bed and Breakfast Accommodations – St. Catharines & Region; Dr. Laurel Reid, Brock University; Deborah Pratt, Inniskillin Wines; Bob Kuhns, Vision Niagara; Christine Jones, Niagara Peninsula Conservation Authority; George Bailey, Niagara Parks Commission; Marjorie Ruddy, Niagara Falls Canada Visitor & Convention Bureau; Harley Smith, St. Lawrence Seaway Authority.

We are also grateful to many, many others who have provided support.

Photo Credits

We would like to thank the following organizations and individuals for giving us permission to use their photographs in this book:

Thies Bogner
Claudette Losier
Niagara Falls, Canada Visitor & Convention Bureau
Niagara Falls (Ontario) Public Library
Niagara Parks Commission
Niagara Peninsula Conservation Authority
St. Catharines Historical Museum
Wine Council of Ontario

Credit is given to the appropriate organization/individual along the side of each photograph. Where no credit is given, the photograph was taken by the authors. The photograph on the front cover was taken by Hans Tammemagi. The photograph on the back cover, sunset at Long Beach Conservation Area, was kindly provided by the Niagara Peninsula Conservation Authority. Copyright remains with the organization or individual credited for the photograph.

About The Authors

Hans is an environmental consultant, free-lance writer, and adjunct professor at Brock University. He grew up in St. Catharines, Ontario. Allyson is a registered nurse and long-time resident of the Niagara area. They live in St. Catharines and spend much of their free time exploring Niagara.

Other books by Hans Tammemagi:
Winning Proposals: How to write them and get results
Landfills, Incinerators, and the Waste Crisis: The search for a sustainable future

To Order This Book

Copies of this book may be purchased at many bookstores and retail outlets. It may also be ordered by mail within Canada by sending $18.50 plus $3.50 for taxes, shipping and handling per book to Oakhill Publishing House. If ordering from the USA send $14.25 (US) plus $3.00 (US) per book.

Oakhill Publishing House
P.O. Box 22012, Glenridge Plaza
St. Catharines, Ontario L2T 4C1
(905) 641-2732 Fax: (905) 641-1705
oakhill@vaxxine.com